NIGEL JENKINS
Damned for Dreaming
and other essays

Foreword by Ali Anwar
and Jon Gower

H'Mm

Cover photo by Branwen Jenkins
Typeset and designed by Andy Dark
Printed in Wales by Gwasg Gomer, Llandysul

Published by the H'mm Foundation,
Grove Extension — Room 426, Swansea University,
Singleton Park, Swansea, SA2 8PP

Contents

Acknowledgements

Acknowledgement is due to Nigel Jenkins' literary executors:
Angharad Jenkins, Margot Morgan and Branwen Jenkins.
Also to *Planet, Wales Arts Review, Poetry Wales, The Guardian,
The Independent, The Institute of Welsh Affairs, Plaid Cymru,
WalesOnline* and *BBC Radio Four.*
We are grateful to Branwen Jenkins for allowing us to use her
photograph of Nigel Jenkins for the cover.
We are also grateful to Siân Edwards for her diligence and
constructive recommendations for improvements to the text.
We would like to thank Sarah Hill and Jon Gower who took time
to read the proofs and made many valuable suggestions.
And finally, to Andy Dark for putting this volume together.

Foreword

Saying and Essaying

Ali Anwar and Jon Gower

A writer has a choice of forms to employ and engage. In Nigel Jenkins's case he took to the travelogue with his award-winning *Gwalia in Khasia*, produced volume after volume of poetry of distinction, churned out reams of journalism, probed the limits, or more properly the depths of psychogeography, not to mention helping to arrange the compendiousness of an encyclopaedia. But he clearly had both a soft spot and high regard for the essay form, which helped him explore and present subjects as wide-ranging as fellow poet John Tripp's wake, the waves of Welsh history, visual art, the lives of favourite musicians, and detailing his spell in prison after refusing to pay a fine following a CND protest.

This collection brings together some of his most engaging essays, ranging in subject matter from the regeneration of Swansea's copper belt and its shiny SA1 waterfront through the unsung art of Evan Walters to the lost and forgotten farms of Gower. As you might expect, he writes about poetry, such as his beloved haiku, and about poets too, so here we find insightful profiles of the likes of Childe Roland, Adrian Mitchell, Christine Evans, David Cobb and Idris Davies, the last of these being a lifelong influence on his own poetry making. Collectively they underline his gifts for prose which often matched those for poetry — all evidencing a curious mind and a writer equipped with a packed toolbook, stuffed to the brim with alert language and pertinent ideas.

Damned for Dreaming also gathers assorted writings — some of them published for the first time here — including Nigel's Top Ten songs and a haunting vignette of his father, first broadcast on Radio 4. There is also a selection of obituaries and tributes which remind us not only what we have lost with his passing but also what we were given by him. Here are assembled some of the thoughts and insights of a man who was generous to a fault.

The *Oxford Dictionary of Literary Terms* defines the essay as "a short written composition in prose that discusses a subject or proposes an argument without claiming to be a complete or thorough exposition. A minor literary form, the essay is more relaxed than the formal academic exposition."

That last phrase certainly seems to apply to Nigel's forays into the form. He was anything but a formal academic, even though he worked at Swansea University and helped create, with Stevie Davies, its burgeoning creative writing department. But to say he wasn't an academic does not mean his writing was without rigour, or fact checking. His early years as a newspaper journalist had taught him the value of notebook, direct quotation and probing towards the truth. Indeed one of his mantras for students was to keep a writer's journal about them at all times and it could be quite disconcerting when he would start taking notes in the middle of a conversation. Yet this allowed him to "catch a moment on the wing," as Stevie Davies put it in her essay about Nigel in the memorial volume *Encounters with Nigel,* also published by the H'mm Foundation. And while he bristled at the bureaucratic slog of academia he was also a simply brilliant teacher — encouraging to a fault, supportive of students to an extent that made him almost everybody's personal tutor. And that teacherly quality is there in the essays: here is a man who wants to share what he has learned and wants the reader to experience what he has experienced, even as he makes language sing with all the care he reserved for his old blues' harmonica.

The H'mm Foundation is pleased to share Nigel's prose with those who have long enjoyed his work as well as introduce his voice to a new generation, just as we were blessed in great measure to have known him as a friend.

Nigel Jenkins

Blindfold in the land of our birth

Nigel Jenkins
25/25 Vision: Welsh horizons across 50 years

"Wales," Harri Webb declared in *Planet* in 1976, "is marching backwards into independence, everybody desperately pretending that we are going somewhere else." Although this pronouncement was typical of the extravagant optimism to which Harri was sometimes given, I hoped he might be right. Then came the crashing disappointment of the four-to-one defeat for devolution in the 1979 referendum, which stunned many a patriot into numb silence. Wales didn't seem to be marching anywhere, but lurching blindfold in ever-decreasing circles. "No day like this for 700 years," lamented the poets Jon Dressel and T. James Jones, raw with political grief, in a poem which compared the outcome of the 1 March referendum with the murder of Llywelyn ap Gruffudd in 1282 and the snuffing out of Welsh independence.[1] Yet here we are in 2012, getting used to mouthing deeply satisfying expressions such as 'the Welsh government' without needing a reality pinch to wake us from idle fantasy. What has happened in little more than thirty years? What in our present "interesting times" might be going to happen?

The poet John Tripp spoke for many when, in an interview in December 1979, he declared:

> "What happened on March the first is a tragedy. It's not a hiccup as Harri Webb said ... It's awful what happened on March the first, and you can't expect your poets to be the same again. You spend ten or twelve years of your life working up to something, with all the irony and cynicism, with all the beating of breasts, you've had these great

hopes for your country ... It's ridiculous."[2]

Some more or less gave up on a Wales that seemed bereft of backbone. For instance, the political commentator Patrick Hannan suggested that Wales no longer had a politics worthy of comment. But certain "tired old valiants", in the words of Tripp's poem 1.III.79, refusing to be defeated by defeat, came

limping through the smoke,
[got] patched up and mended,
then [went] back up the line again.

What beckoned for some was, in Dafydd Elis-Thomas's words, "the long march through the institutions", an unglamorous but necessary engagement with the nation's policymakers in the fields of business, economics, local government, education and the media. Two of the most resourceful and energetic activists on that front were the writer and journalist John Osmond (who has been Director of the Institute of Welsh Affairs since 1996) and his friend the journalist Robin Reeves (1941-2001). Shortly before the foundation of the IWA in 1987, they launched the St David's Forum that in many respects anticipated the purpose and functions of the IWA. "I was prompted to embark on the initiative by a trip I went on to speak at a conference in Quebec in the wake of the '79 referendum," John told me. "The conference was organised by the University of Quebec at Montreal to debate their forthcoming referendum in late 1979. I struck up a conversation with some people from the Parti Québécois and they asked me whether the business community had been supportive of the Welsh referendum ... ! Ah, they replied, you'll get nowhere in Wales until you mobilise a significant section of the business community."

With sponsorship from business and industry, John and Robin

organised two or three forums a year, in large hotels in different parts of Wales and on various themes. I attended several of these well-fed and bibulous gatherings as the forum's official scribe. My job was to turn my wine-splashed shorthand into a 5,000-word summary of the discussions — which participants were assured would be non-attributable, to encourage 'a frank and unfettered' exchange of views. *Y Cynefin*, that numinous and untranslatable term meaning, roughly, 'native ground', was the topic for the inaugural St David's Forum, held at the Bulkeley Hotel, Beaumaris. It involved contributions from several authorities steeped in the matter of Wales, among them the author and chief executive of Gwynedd County Council, Ioan Bowen Rees (1929-99) and the scholar Bedwyr Lewis Jones (1933-92). But there was also a sprinkling of lost souls, chiefly from the world of business, who had hardly a clue where they were. If they thought of Wales at all they thought of it as some western county of England. There was almost 'an international incident' at the Friday night dinner when the assembly was invited to stand and raise glasses to Dewi Sant, rather than the Queen. Who or what was this Dewi Sant, a couple of flustered businessmen angrily enquired, fearing that they were being bamboozled into toasting Meibion Glyndŵr, the arsonists of holiday and second homes who were much in the news at the time.

The St David's Forum continued to meet until the mid 1990s, when it ceded the field to Geraint Talfan Davies's slightly younger but professionally staffed and funded IWA. By then, thanks in part to the lead taken by the think-tanks, talk of such entities as 'the Welsh economy' had become normal, whereas a decade earlier such particularisation would have seemed to more UK-centred sensibilities both eccentric and strange. Similarly today, thanks to the strengthening of national civic identity and to the development of a new corpus of Welsh law, we are beginning to talk of a Welsh legal system.

The be-suited revolutionaries embroiled in "the long march through the institutions" have been acutely aware of the inadequacies of both the education system and the print and broadcasting media in nurturing a sense of Welsh citizenship. Most Welsh people have a poor grasp of their history and, given the shortcomings of the media, few are prepared to invest the conscious effort that is necessary to keep abreast of Welsh current affairs. "You would say / this place deserved better / if you knew ..." wrote John Tripp in *The Province of Belief*. With an understanding of both past and present largely beyond their reach, many of our compatriots are unlikely to make a sufficiently informed contribution to the construction of a national future. It is gratifying, indeed, that under such circumstances a comfortable majority voted, in March 2011, in favour of law-making powers for the National Assembly. With 21 out of 22 local authority areas voting yes, the Welsh showed themselves united politically for the first time in centuries.

Whenever I'm in Ireland or Scotland I find myself casting an envious eye over national newspapers such as the *Irish Times* or the *Scotsman*, which hum with brio and bristle with an intelligence sadly lacking in our own distinctly provincial "national newspaper". Why are the weak-beer Welsh so fond of watering down ambitious projects? Another nation-building venture of John Osmond and co., alongside his promotion of a thoroughgoing Welsh Baccalaureate (which would eventually suffer a thorough drenching by the champions of mediocrity) was *Wales on Sunday*, launched in March 1989, which everyone was expecting to be a *Welsh Observer*. Invited to be the paper's literary editor, I spent several months leading up to the paper's launch preparing dummy versions of a books page. What the paper as a whole looked like the workers were not allowed to know. Presumably to foil any attempt at industrial sabotage, the dummies were kept largely unseen in a safe in the then-editor John Humphries' office. When the first edition eventually appeared, those of us who'd imagined, with mounting excitement, that we were preparing a Welsh Sunday broadsheet of substance were sorely disappointed. But still, we thought, it's a start: onwards and upwards from here. But downwards dumbingly *Wales on Sunday* slid, getting increasingly superficial and excitable by the week.

Why, I wondered after months of declining standards in pursuit of rising sales, did they still want a books page? Then came a coup at the palace. I picked up the paper one Sunday morning to find my choice of books and reviewers replaced by books I'd never have chosen, by reviewers I'd never heard of, on footballers, pop stars, showbiz and war, and nothing whatsoever from or about Wales. It was Thomson House's way of telling Jenkins he was sacked. More recently, Ned Thomas's bruising experience of trying to launch a daily newspaper in Welsh, *Y Byd*, underlines the difficulties facing those who aspire to publish an intelligent, properly national newspaper in either language. With almost all newspaper sales declining sharply, it seems that we must look for compensatory developments in radio, television and online services. Yet how specifically Welsh news and cultural debate might thrive in such media remains to be seen, unless the issue is taken more seriously by the Welsh government than it has been so far.

If you knew, if you only knew ... Education, the media, canny networking: how are the people of Wales to *get* Wales — or to *want* to get Wales? I know from my own experience what a long and difficult journey it can be from Welshness by default, because you were born in Wales but don't know or care much about it, to an informed engagement with the country. I want to see Wales break free from its stifling dependency on England, to use its abundant talents and natural resources to transform the lives of its people, many of whom live in appalling poverty, and to engage directly, on its own terms, with other nations, making itself useful in the world.

It was as an adolescent, at a horse trials event on the estate of

Captain Peter Francis near Llandeilo, that I first caught a glimpse of Welsh nationalism. "See that man over there?" the host's daughter asked me. "That's Cayo Evans. He believes Wales should be an independent country." This struck me, as an apolitical hedonist in the making, as the strangest of strange notions. I had never heard of the Free Wales Army or Plaid Cymru or Saunders Lewis or R.S. Thomas. Dylan Thomas ("Land of my fathers — my fathers can keep it") was my poet, not that I could understand much of his arcane word-spinning. Welshness, I'd probably have thought, was a retarding affliction best left behind in the 19th Century. Most of my family had been in anxious denial of their Welshness for two generations. The Meurigs, Eluneds, Eiras and Dilyses of my grandparents' era had given way in my parents' time to names such as Ian, Roger, Noel, and Rowland, as chapel and the Welsh language had been abandoned for church and English. The farmers and steelworkers of the family's past had magicked themselves into white-bread bourgeois with a penchant for the English public school.

I had never heard, either, of Meic Stephens, Harri Webb and others who, around that time, at Garth Newydd in Merthyr Tydfil, were busily hatching *Poetry Wales*, the magazine that would spearhead a radical redirection of the literary climate. And it was literature, poetry above all, that would eventually hand me the key to Wales. Other factors also played a role: living and working (as a newspaper reporter) in England, and looking anew, from a distance, at a Wales I'd barely begun to comprehend; the questions asked me about my country by Americans, Canadians, Greeks, Italians, Germans, Spaniards, Moroccans as I bummed and odd-jobbed my way around mainland Europe and north Africa for a year or so; the questions I asked myself about Wales as I skimped my official studies at Essex University to immerse myself in the Welsh magazines, especially *Planet*, and the writings of Gwyn Williams

(Trefenter), Idris Davies, David Jones, Harri Webb, John Tripp, Tony Conran. I even wrote an essay on Dafydd ap Gwilym — of whom no one in the Department of European and Comparative Literature had heard.

We are used to Wales being invisible in the wider world. But it's Wales's relative invisibility to large numbers of the Welsh themselves that has been so impoverishing of both individual and civic identity. I speak as one of the many — perhaps the majority — of those born thus blindfold to the land of their birth, its history and culture, and I am all too aware of what a strenuous and convoluted effort it took to peel that blindfold from my eyes. It was most revealing, during the 1997 devolution campaign, how the 'Yes' camp was able to draw on contributions from any number of poets and musicians to hearten and entertain the devolutionary troops, whereas the joyless 'No' moaners, seemingly bereft of any cultural underpinning and ignorant of their country's arts, could call on no choirs, rock bands, bards or folk singers to support their curmudgeonly cause.

By the time I graduated in 1976, I knew, after the best part of a decade in 'exile', that I wanted to return not simply to live in Wales but to inhabit Wales as fully as possible and to make some kind of contribution to Welsh life. Not all patriots have enjoyed the luxury of a long period of literary and historical reflection to wake them up to Wales. For some in the early 1960s it was the high-handed flooding of Cwm Celyn by the Liverpool Corporation that alerted them to Welsh impotence. For others it was Margaret Thatcher's nasty and brutish 1980s — which, as things turned out, would prove the making of Welsh devolution — it's presumably why a giant tin portrait of the woman hangs in the Senedd in Cardiff Bay. Similarly today, David Cameron and co. are making an invaluable contribution to the maturation of Welsh nationhood.

Most of my family, although content to call themselves Welsh, remain vague about national specifics, and can be relied upon to vote no — if they vote at all — to any measure that might advance the cause of Welsh autonomy and self-respect. They didn't join me on my protracted and intriguing journey of Welsh discovery. On the other hand, my two daughters are inheritors of some of the treasures I picked up along the way. They have the courage of an informed, bilingual, easy-going Welshness which fits them to embrace with enthusiasm the prospect of a Wales at last free, in the foreseeable future, after more than 700 years of being England's first colony.

I have not expected to see an independent Wales in my lifetime, even when most extravagantly 'surprised by wine'. But these 'interesting times' could surprise us all. It's not impossible that by the time of their independence referendum in 2014 the Scots could summon the gumption to vote Yes to regaining their independence. The consequent shock to Wales of finding itself more outnumbered than ever by a congenitally Tory-voting England in the rump state of "Little Britain" could concentrate Welsh political thinking dramatically, offering definitive proof of the folly of remaining in a grotesquely unequal union with a polity fundamentally at odds with Welsh communitarian practices and aspirations.

The vote of confidence in devolution delivered by the electorate in March 2011 suggests that already the Welsh are beginning to get that message. Although at present fewer than 10 per cent of the population, according to the polls, favour independence, growing numbers of people seem increasingly receptive to greater self-determination for Wales, as they appreciate the improvements made in their lives by high-profile Welsh Government measures such as free prescriptions and safeguarding the NHS, bus passes for the over-sixties, and subsidised education for students. As more people wake up to the fact that Wales is energy rich, with abundant natural resources, particularly water, the prospect of detachment from a spendthrift and deeply indebted state that wastes billions on nuclear weapons, illegal wars, a parasitic monarchy and bloated sporting circuses, may not seem such a romantic and unfeasible indulgence.

Whether or not Scotland votes to regain its independence, the process of Welsh devolution will continue. Europe, in spite of the constant anti-EU propaganda of the media and many politicians, is likely to become increasingly important, as will our relationships with neighbouring Celtic countries and other members of the European Free Alliance who aspire to full national self-determination. The relationship with England will sooner or later need to be "reset". Much will depend on how England's regions negotiate their own democratic deficit and how England, long blinded by the dazzle of empire, reawakens to the particularities of its own nationhood. Let's hope that the version it chooses for itself is the England of Shakespeare, the Levellers and the Diggers, Tom Paine, William Blake, Charles Dickens, the *Guardian*, Adrian Mitchell and P.J. Harvey, rather than that of the football hooligan, the English Defence League and the British National Party.

Until Wales regains its long-lost independence we should live the Wales we want. The socialist republic of Cymru is the land in which I and many others have been living for years. Come and join us.

INSTITUTE OF WELSH AFFAIRS (IWA) - SEPTEMBER 2012

1. The poem, *Ianws*, came close to winning the Crown at the 1979 National Eisteddfod, but was disqualified when it was revealed that the poem had two authors. Some have claimed that while this was the official reason for the poem being denied the Crown, the real reason was that the poem bristled with too many painful home truths.
2. Quoted from 'An Interview with John Tripp' conducted by Nigel Jenkins and edited for *Planet* 60, December-January 1986-87.

Ghost Farms

*Nigel Jenkins on the Gower peninsula's
agricultural crisis*

Cocklebushes, Deer Park, The Lawn, Six Acres, Poppins Park, The Leg... Just an odd list of names; but to me, these field names are among the most resonantly evocative and poignant words I know. To dwell on them is to conjure from the drizzles of forgetfulness both a green-and-golden childhood and a farm not untypical of the dozens of Gower farms which in recent decades have been blown chaff-like into oblivion by "market forces".

If it's true that you are not fully dead until your name has been spoken on earth for the very last time, then the ability of the remaining survivors of Kilvrough Park Farm (my brother, my sister, my mother and me) to name all its fields assures the old farm, for a few years more, of a spectral existence in our imaginations. But, having been sold off piecemeal, like so many others, the farm now has half a dozen different owners, not one of whom is likely to know the names of the few fields he owns, let alone the names of neighbouring plots, all of which once cohered, under a single family's ownership, as 120 acres of prime agricultural land, with a history, a personality, a culture. As a farm divested of its names, its unity and all productive purpose, the place no longer makes sense. All that's produced here are appearances: the vague look of a farm; a field striped by chain-harrows to resemble a suburban lawn; the conspicuously indulgent trappings of horsiculture. And to look like a bit of a farmer, because you've bought a field or two and a barn or a shed, would seem to be enough to entitle you to build a house on your "farm" — which has been for many a nifty circumvention of the Area of Outstanding Natural Beauty's supposedly stringent planning regulations. Where once there was a single farmhouse in the midst of a working farm, there may now be a rash of "farmhouses" — of boxy or grandiloquently pretentious design, with rootless names, pseudo-Victorian lampposts and defensive electric gates — dotting the pathetically redundant fields.

Kilvrough's situation is far from unique. In an area of roughly 2 square kilometers, bounded by Southgate and Parkmill to the west, Fairwood Common to the north, Bishopston to the east, and the coast to the south, there once thrived, until well into the 1970s, at least a dozen farms, in addition to the twenty market gardens of Bishopston. The market gardens long ago disappeared, and there are now only two or three fully functioning farms. The rest have been sold off in dribs and drabs — a field here, two fields there — as incomes have diminished, debts have mounted and younger generations have forsaken the land for a better living elsewhere (myself, *mea culpa*, among them). It's a pattern repeated throughout Gower: by 2008, there were fewer than ten dairy farms left in the entire peninsula, and only about four farms growing the famed Gower potato. My brother, who enjoys a much higher standard of living as an agricultural estate agent than he could have achieved as a farmer, says he hasn't sold a whole farm in Gower for years: "When a farmer decides to call it a day, he knows that market conditions determine that he'll get a far better deal for himself by selling his land off in bits and pieces — even though, sadly, that will mean the end of the farm as a going concern. I can't see that there will ever be a way of putting these pieces back together again to make viable farms."

It was the quality of its farmland that first attracted the Normans to south Gower — its loamy brown-earth soils, its well-drained limestone base, its favourable and relatively frost-free climate; and there remain one or two names on the home patch which can be read as bitter souvenirs of the invaders' drive to wrest the land out of Welsh hands and to resist native attempts to regain control. One of the few Welsh place names in the parish of Pennard is that of a ruined farmhouse, Pwll-y-bloggi (resort of the wolf dog), which would seem to record a battle against the Normans on 15 April, 1136, after which packs of wolves descended from the hills to feast on the bodies of the 516 men killed in the conflict. Then there is that curious name, Kilvrough. My parents used to joke that it meant "the abode of swine", which I took to be a groundless fancy, until the poet Harri Webb (1920-94) suggested to me that Kilvrough could well be an Anglicisation of cil-yr-hwch (retreat of the sow) — the sow being none other than Llywelyn Fawr (Llywelyn ap Iorwerth, Prince of Wales, c.1173-1240), known hereabouts for the swinish ferocity with which he and his warriors would rout up everything that stood in their path.

But it was the invaders who prevailed, consigning the natives to the heavy, damp, acid soils of the north and east, and establishing in the south, around nucleated villages, their manorial system of open fields, divided into strips of an acre or more. The cliff-top walk between Rhossili village and the point passes alongside a substantial tract known as the Vile (or Viel), which retains to this day its medieval open-field layout, with the strips — up to about forty metres wide — bounded by low grassy banks known as landshares. Each strip, intended to be as large as a man could plough in one day, has a name, such as Sandyland, Priest Hay and Bramble Bush. Bishopston too was known for small, elongated fields fashioned originally by the Normans.

While the cliff-tops and commons provided ample grazing for sheep and cattle, the fields were used largely for cultivation. Given the relatively limited dimensions of the peninsula — twenty kilometres long and no more than ten kilometres wide — Gower's farms have been capable of much greater variety than nearby areas. The uplands of Glamorgan, for instance, have been confined largely to sheep rearing, while southern Carmarthenshire has been known mainly for dairying. But all seven main types of farming have been possible in Gower: sheep, dairying, beef and mixed livestock, pigs and poultry, cropping, horticulture and — the most common of all — mixed, a sustainable system that endured for centuries.

Most of Gower's open fields, as those elsewhere, underwent enclosure in the eighteenth century. They were worked, particularly in south Gower, largely by tenant farmers who paid their dues to the big estate owners, chief among them the Talbots of Penrice, the Lucases of Stouthall, and the Dawkinses (and subsequently the Penrices and Lyonses) of Kilvrough. The demise of the big estates, a process which began with the break-up of Kilvrough in 1919 and ended with the sale of Clyne and Parc le Breos in the 1950s, represented a liberation for the peninsula's tenant farmers. Many bought their farms at highly favourable rates, and most were relieved that they were no longer answerable to representatives of a sometimes autocratic ancien régime.

The dispersal of the 4000-acre Kilvrough Estate gave my grandfather, T.E. (Tom) Jenkins, who had been the Lyonses' agent, the opportunity to acquire his own farm. He bought the estate's home farm, Kilvrough Farm, opposite Kilvrough Manor, and began his farming life during a period of considerable change. New varieties of grasses were being experimented with, and potato growing and mixed farming burgeoned. The advent of mechanised transport in 1922 enabled the easy and rapid transit of crops and livestock to markets in Swansea and further afield. The installation of piped water supplies encouraged increased milk production. The mid-1930s saw the first Fordson tractors arriving in Gower, while the government introduced the first in a long series of measures to subsidise agricultural production, lending a degree of security to a way of life which, for centuries, had been hard and precarious.

Becoming surer of their future, many farmers grew land hungry;

their expansionism introduced an element of fluidity in land boundaries which, for generations, had remained the same. Tom Jenkins eventually fancied a bigger farm, and so decamped to Kilvrough Park Farm on the other side of the road (the A4118 south Gower road). The farm, in due course, was inherited by my father, and this was where my siblings and I were raised.

Ours was a typical mixed farm. We had a herd of about twenty milking cows and twenty or so beef cattle, a small flock of sheep, half a dozen pigs, some chickens, a few ducks and sometimes geese. We grew hay, barley, oats, wheat, potatoes, swedes, mangolds (for feeding the cattle) and, in a kitchen garden, beans, peas, cabbages, sprouts and salad vegetables, largely for our own consumption. We shot pigeons, rabbits and the odd hare. The rationing imposed during the Second World War continued well into the 1950s, but we were hardly aware of it, because, like most other Gower farming families at that time, we were more or less self-sufficient in food.

Farming, of this traditional kind, represented not just a living but a way of life. The farm whose recent fragmentation has rendered it meaningless was once instinct with meaning. It nourished our present, proposed a future, and connected us, in disparate ways, with a sense of the past which encompassed elements ranging from the intimately personal to the distantly international. Bounded by three roads and a wooded ridge, it formed, roughly, a square patch of fields, akin to the milltir sgwar, the cosily familiar "square mile" of Welsh rural tradition, set within the wider home locality of the bro, which embraced neighbouring farms and nearby villages.

In the corner of the farm's south-easternmost field, Church Park, is the (possibly) fourteenth-century Pennard Church, where the family were christened, married and buried, and where the few believers among us regularly worshipped, while the rest ignored the tolling across our fields of the church's mournful bell. Harri Webb is buried here, and there's a plaque inside the church commemorating the poet Vernon Watkins (1906-1967) who lived on the cliffs at Pennard and worshipped in this church. In the south-western corner of Church Park, and at the southern end of Poppins Park, was Kilvrough Cottage — now extended and uPVC-ed out of recognition — where my paternal great-grandfather lived. I still have the remains of the pocketwatch that the widowed and dilapidated old farmer used to take to pieces, and dreamily shove back together again, to pass the time in his last long days.

In the farm's south-westernmost corner was an area of Deer Park known as Quarry Field, after the small, disused quarry that lurked beneath a fringe of scrubby trees. What buildings of limestone were quarried for here, I have often wondered — the church, the farm's cowshed, our house, with the date of its construction, 1886, over the porch?

At the north-western edge of our "square world" was Kilvrough Manor, a youth hostel in the 1950s and now an outward-bound centre owned by Oxfordshire Education Committee, but formerly the manorial hub of a great Gower estate, and a player in events of high drama and some exoticism. It was from here that Major Thomas Penrice, the squire of Kilvrough, led about thirty men of the Swansea and Fairwood Corps of Yeomen Cavalry to engage, somewhat ineffectually, with the armed insurrectionists of Merthyr Tydfil, during the Merthyr Rising of 1831; the major and his men seem to have spent much of the encounter in a pub at Aberpergwm. And then there was the visit to Kilvrough of the Emperor of Abyssinia, Haile Selassie, descendant of King Solomon and the Queen of Sheba, and the black messiah of the Rastafarian faith. My grandmother remembered meeting him there, perhaps when his son, Prince Lidi Asrate Kasa, was a pupil at the Bible College School, Blackpill, during the early years of the Second World War. She also handed on the story of an attempt, in 1809, to commit suttee at the manor, by the part-Indian widow of another military owner of

Kilvrough, Major William Crompton Green of the East India Company. Following Major Green's death, his distraught widow was determined to burn herself alive along with the body of her husband on a funeral pyre on the lawn, in accordance with Hindu custom. Mrs Green's proposal horrified the locals, and it was only by the most strenuous exertions that she was persuaded against self-immolation, eventually allowing her husband to be buried in Pennard churchyard.

It's clear from any map that the main south Gower road used to go straight past the front door of Kilvrough Manor, but when the estate was being freshly landscaped in the eighteenth century the road was diverted in a dramatic loop to the north. Its teetering wall — the bane of motorists unused to Gower's wayward roads — is topped with triangular coping blocks cast from copper slag produced at the Vivians' Hafod (Swansea) copper works.

The same kind of blue-black slag blocks top the garden wall of the Round House at the farm's north-easterly corner. My grandmother, who lived there for many years, used to explain that an earlier version of the house was indeed round, and that it had been built in about 1840 to control a turnpike toll-gate — of the kind which so infuriated the hard-pressed small farmers of south-west Wales that, as the Daughters of Rebecca, they rose against their oppressors, attacking the hated toll-gates and ultimately forcing the abolition of the turnpike trusts. In 1843, Rebecca had "visited" and entirely destroyed the Pound-ffald toll-gate in Three Crosses a couple of miles away. They were thought to have the Kilvrough toll-gate in their sights, and special constables were deployed at the Round House, but there were no further Rebecca visitations in Gower.

Some of the fields names — Cocklebushes, Poppins Park — defy explanation, although, for me, they are as evocative of the acres they describe as is the "abstract" name of a dear friend. Some are self-explanatory: the high-walled and stoutly hedged Stallion Paddock;

or The Orchard, with a meagre scattering of aged apple and pear trees where once there would have been scores in carefully tended rows. Many names probably originated during the period of busy field creation inaugurated by the enclosure acts of the eighteenth century, and several — The Lawn, Deer Park — characterise the artfully planned parkland so beloved of the eighteenth- and nineteenth-century gentry. In the walled Tower Field, where we kept pigs (and where, in 2008, pigs were again being raised), there was a classic parkland folly, a circular tower which had once had two storeys, but was now open to the sky, its flooring long decayed. As a romantic teenager, I used to fantasise (with W.B. Yeats in mind) about restoring the tower and secluding myself there — with wine, books and a beautiful girl — to compose poetry. One poem I wanted to write — and have yet to do so — concerned the white owl which used to live in the tower, and which used to fascinate my infant father when his mother took him on walks there. One day they found the owl lying dead in the tall grass at the foot of the tower; someone had shot it.

The Second World War made its mark. The manor was used as a billet for troops, and one or two asbestos nissen huts were erected on the farm, perhaps in connection with the aerodrome (1941) that was constructed, in some desperation, on Fairwood Common. One of these huts, tucked in behind the manor, was later the home of the cowman and his family, and I lived there myself for some years in the 1970s. Until the aerodrome was completed, there was a landing strip on what we called Watkinses' fields — after the Watkins family of Widegate, who rented the land from us. Those fields must have had older names, but clearly they were lost during our tenure of the farm, thanks to our carelessness — just as the remaining names that were transmitted to us down the generations are unknown to the land's latest owners. Cocklebushes, for instance, has become the Gower Riding Club Field. The entire farm, bereft of its traditional names and of all familial and historic associations, could be renamed Terra Incognita.

I walked the old farm guiltily in June this year (2008) — the guilt occasioned not by my trespassing, but by the uncomfortable recognition that my abdication, as a fugitive teenager, of what could have been a birthright had played no small part in the farm's eventual demise. The mewing in this wilderness of a lone buzzard provided a mournful accompaniment as I tramped through ungrazed thicknesses of grass, and struggled in vain — through swathes of shoulder-high nettle, thistle and bramble pushing deep into the fields from untended hedgerows — to find old gateways into the woods, which were now unmanaged, impenetrable jungles. Familiar lines of connection from field to (clogged) pond to woodland path were obstructed at every turn by the barbed-wired, wasteful untidiness of it all. The place was like an abandoned student flat in which no one had washed any dishes for years.

There are similar ghost farms throughout the peninsula. Like farmers elsewhere in Wales, those of Gower have had to contend with a seemingly limitless onslaught of impediments and disincentives, from the crises of BSE ("mad cow disease"), foot-and-mouth disease, bovine tuberculosis and various food scares, to tidal waves of form-filling and bureaucracy, and the crippling expense of items such as machinery, chemical fertilisers and fuel. Most farmers work more than 60 hours a week, yet incomes have fallen by over 50 per cent since 1995: all too often, they end up selling the food they produce for less than it costs them to produce it. Fifty cows would once have been considered a sizeable herd, but these days — with supermarket milk being cheaper than bottled water — the dairy farmer needs about 300 milkers to have a chance of survival. Then there's globalisation: the capitalist madness (and rank immorality) of using virtual slave labour in "developing" countries to rear poor-quality animals (and other foodstuffs), in conditions that would be illegal here, for meat that is shipped half way round the world and sold to us over-fed dupes at knock-down prices in the local supermarket — while thousands of children in those countries die every day of starvation and malnutrition.

No human activity is more important than the production of food. Although life for most Gower farmers has never been easy, they worked their land resourcefully for centuries, to produce not only an abundance of food but a society and a culture, which have been in serious decline for decades. With the ending of automatic subsidies after 2013, the future for agriculture has never looked more uncertain. The ruination of Gower's farms seems doomed to continue, and for many there would seem to be no alternative. But sooner or later, it seems to me, the worsening global food crisis will reach such a desperate pitch as to enforce — let's hope without recourse to military coercion — the social ownership of productive land: for the production, once again, of the staple of life.

PLANET 191

Across the Tawe's Great Divide

One of the biggest urban regeneration projects in Europe, Swansea's £200m SA1 development, is transforming the city's dockland, with the intention of making Swansea a waterfront city of international importance.

"Swansea, in point of spirit, fashion, and politeness," declared *The Gloucester Journal* in 1786, "has now become the Brighton of Wales." Equipping itself with all the trappings of a refined and stylish place of resort — pleasure gardens, bathing machines, circulating libraries, theatres, public assembly rooms and a newspaper — Swansea might indeed, at that juncture, have taken the seaside route to genteel (if relatively modest) prosperity. But coalmining and the smelting of lead, zinc and copper were already gathering implacable momentum in the Lower Swansea Valley, and Swansea was well on its way to becoming "Copperopolis", the metallurgical capital of the world, with steel and tinplate destined to supplant copper as major forces in the local economy. So, eighteenth-century Swansea chose the industrial route, to vastly greater wealth (for some) than might have strewed the seaside path, and the Brighton option remained the road not taken. By the mid twentieth century, Swansea's 200-year industrial bacchanal had given way to a seemingly incurable hangover, in the form of the most derelict and polluted landscape — in the Lower Swansea Valley — of any in Britain.

The road not taken looked like the road beyond repair. But as Swansea muddled through yet another of its periodic identity crises, the worst of that post-industrial squalor was gradually cleared away (along with a lamentable quantity of Swansea's historic industrial architecture), and the seaside path beckoned once more. The first steps along that route were tentative. The elongated triangle of seafront Swansea once known as the Burrows, stretching from what is now the Dylan Thomas Centre beside the Tawe to westerly Brynmill, had been the modish heartland of polite, early nineteenth-century society. But by about the 1850s — when the South Dock was carved out of the very core of the Burrows, and railway lines were laid down the middle of elegant Georgian streets — commerce and industry had overwhelmed the area. By the time the dock closed in 1969, most of the former Burrows had fallen into abandonment and ruin, and the council wondered what to do with the dried out, rubbish filled sump. A dual carriageway? A sunken garden? An estate of municipal housing? Executive luxury bungalows? Then somebody noticed, winking beyond the southern retaining wall, the sea — which the authorities promptly let back in to the dock. They began to address not a problem but an opportunity. By the late 1980s, Swansea's transformed maritime quarter was attracting international awards and setting a possible precedent for the increasingly run-down dockland on the other side of the Tawe, across which the spoils of freshly affluent Swansea had so far failed to find a way. The challenge was how to use the sea and the river to unite a city long divided between smug middle-class west and working-class east. When the Tawe barrage was completed in 1992 — Britain's first tidal barrage across a river — a pedestrian walkway across the barrage failed to materialise, as did a suggested river-boat service and the housing, leisure and new commercial opportunities that had been promised for the eastside.

Nothing much happened for a decade. Then in 2003, seemingly overnight, Swansea found itself with a startling new landmark, visible for miles, the architecturally exuberant Sail Bridge for pedestrians and cyclists. What was all this about? Swansea didn't do "modern". Swansea had run a mile from Will Allsop's audacious design for a national literature centre in the early 1990s (which he later recycled, to international acclaim, as Peckham's new library), preferring the cosy familiarity of the outmoded, the second-hand and the make-do-and-mend. The £2m Sail Bridge, with its 42-metre mast, was intended as a fanfare of revolutionary intent, trumpeting the inauguration of the SA1 Swansea waterfront development, declaring the project's unabashed contemporaneity and proposing an end to the historic east/west divide.

The £200m, WDA-managed SA1 project, which will take at least ten more years to complete, is at the forefront of the National Assembly's plan to boost the burgeoning watersports sector by 40 per cent, increasing the sector's annual contribution to the Welsh economy to £224m by 2010. SA1's 400-berth marina, in the 10.9-hectare Prince of Wales Dock, will nearly double the city's mooring capacity, bringing the total number of berths to over 1000, and making Swansea, in terms of capacity, the sailing capital of Wales. The dock will shortly be sold to the WDA by its current owners, Associated British Ports (ABP), for a nominal £1. The 40.47 hectares of semi-derelict land around the dock will sprout tree-lined boulevards, streets and squares, with apartment blocks and houses, underground and multi-storey car parking, offices, businesses, bars, restaurants, a hospital (private), a church (evangelical), extensive leisure and marine facilities, and public art. "SA1 represents an extension eastward of the city centre," project surveyor Leigh Jenkins told me. "Everything you could want for living and working here will be provided, so that in theory you'd never have to leave, if you didn't want to."

Changes at the docks have usually meant changes for Swansea, and vice versa. The commercial port's high visibility at the city's eastern gateway tends to nurture the assumption that the eastside is where Swansea's docks began. Hindsight suggests that they should have begun there, but they didn't. The river itself is where the first quaysides were built, some of which are still robustly present. The problem of vessels having to lie on river mud when the tide was out led to demands for a floating harbour. This was achieved between 1840 and 1852 by excavating a new channel for the Tawe — the New Cut — and using a stretch of the river's original course at the Strand, locked at both ends, to make Swansea's first permanently waterfilled dock, the Town Float or North Dock as it was later known. The North Dock closed in 1928, although its half-tide basin — occupied now by Sainsbury's supermarket — was retained until the early 1960s for ships serving Weaver's Flour Mills.

The decades it took to negotiate and finally construct the Town Float so frustrated the coppermaster John Henry Vivian that he formed a company to build a masonry dock on the Burrows. When the South Dock opened in 1859, it was hailed by *The Cambrian* as "incomparably more important to us, as an industrial and commercial community, than any event that ever transpired in our midst." But it was clear by the 1870s that the two westside docks were unable to keep pace with developments. The eastside's time had come.

The Prince of Wales Dock, which constitutes the hub of SA1, was the first of three to be constructed east of the river — at what was once Fabian's Bay. Opened in 1882, the dock was soon struggling to accommodate the ever-increasing trade and the size of the latest steamships. The Swansea Harbour Trust therefore pushed south into the bay and built the King's Dock, which opened in 1909. A further bulge into the bay resulted in the biggest of Swansea's docks, the Queen's, which opened in 1920, primarily to serve the new oil refinery at Llandarcy.

In Swansea's maritime heyday, there could be as many as a hundred ships massed in the bay, waiting to enter the port. Often enough, these days, there isn't a single freighter to be seen in any of the docks. The only dock with any significant commercial activity is the King's. On a recent visit, there was just one ship moored there, the *Atsuta*, loading coils of Port Talbot steel for China, but there were other cargoes piled on the quaysides awaiting transportation: coal from Tower and Celtic Energy; timber for Finland (strangely); a twinkling mountain of recycled glass for Spain (surely I recognised one or two old Rioja bottles?); used plant from BP Baglan on its way to India. A huge timber warehouse is currently under construction at Robert's Road, and ABP have just invested in a £1.8m fertilizer warehouse on the Graigola Wharf — which is also where Swansea's 200-tonne lock gates are overhauled. There are six gates in active service in the main lock, and four spares, each gate having to be removed for refurbishment every five years. That this is a mighty undertaking for the crane barge *Mersey Mammoth* — which recently failed, initially, to lift one of the gates — is all too apparent when you behold these magnificent, rust-red leviathans reclining in the sun on their wooden chocks. I told my guide, Jon Rees, ABP's safety manager, that their significance to the economy of Swansea prompted me to recast a famous poem by William Carlos Williams: "so much depends/upon/a red lock/gate... 'Everything,' said Jon, 'absolutely everything.'"

At the eastern end of the King's Dock is a compound which, from Fabian Way, looks like a giant toddler's playground, crammed with tops and toys of every hue. This, Trinity House's western headquarters (Harwich covers the east), is where, every five years on a rotational basis, the 484 warning buoys of southern Britain's western seaboard are brought for reconditioning. Trinity House's "west coast manager" is Andy Lamnea — who was born a Swansea man thanks to a happy accident in the 1840s: a Greek seaman happened to be on board one of two ships that collided at Swansea, both of which were then confined to port for repairs; the Greek sailor, kicking his heels around town, fell for a Swansea girl — thus life began to wind its way towards Andy Lamnea. The buoys, Andy explains, are picked up and later repositioned with pinpoint, satellite-navigated accuracy by the Trinity House tender *Mermaid*.

They are hoisted aboard, the bigger, older ones weighing 6 tonnes or more, along with the 50-metre chains that tether them to the "sinkers" — huge bath-plug-like weights (of between 1 and 5 tonnes) — which rest immovably on the sea bottom. The western seaboard, wilder by far than the eastern, has 54 operational lighthouses, which are looked after from Swansea (Harwich services 18). Although serious lifeguarding work is Trinity House's *raison d'être*, it's gratifying to note that that sense of play suggested by initial "tops and toys" impressions is not entirely misplaced. Most establishments desirous of augmenting their dignity with cannon generally plonk one either side of the main portico — not so Trinity House, Swansea, whose portakabin has a single cannon trained directly on the front door, with a wooden mannequin poised to do the explosive honours and a dragon-design cowling over the cannon's mouth which reads "Welsh and thirsty".

Trinity House's repairs yard office nearby was once the superintendent's home. This stocky, red-brick building is one of the oldest structures in the docks, but at least twice its age is a 200-year-old fragment of the original east pier-head — a cracked, house-sized platform of dressed stone sitting forlornly in the river a short distance upstream from where, most days, the Swansea-Cork *Superferry* docks. It was from here, until the early 1920s, that the harbour's one-o'clock gun was fired. While this venerable chunk of old Swansea seems doomed to disappear, along with an adjacent slipway, as SA1 reclaims land in the river mouth, the original lock that linked the Prince of Wales Dock directly to the estuary is to be rescued from rubble-filled oblivion and recommissioned.

Three historic buildings are being painstakingly renovated. The delightful Norwegian Seamen's Church, which moved from Newport in 1910 to a site at the entrance to the docks, has been rebuilt on a site at the heart of SA1, and is destined to play a leading role in a major expansion of Swansea's stained glass industry. It was stored for a while in the second of these refurbished buildings, the so-called J-Shed (all dockside warehouses are named alphabetically), which has been a grain warehouse, a fish market and a general store. One of three restaurant and bar businesses to move into the J-Shed's ground floor is La Basseria, branching out, from its base in Wind Street, with a fish restaurant. The upper floor has been converted into twenty New York-style loft apartments. The third building, earmarked as a fish restaurant, is the Ice House which, with its distinctive chimney stack, is situated near the Sail Bridge. It's a reminder that fishing is the oldest of all Swansea's industries, apart from coalmining. It was built in the 1880s as an ice-making factory for the fishing industry, and it is believed that the freezing floor is still there beneath a later floor. Extended in about 1897, when Swansea was a major deep-fishing port, it became a chandlery in 1926 and then a flag-making factory. These core, historic buildings are complemented by the resolutely contemporary designs of the new offices and blocks of flats, where daring variety rather than harmonisation of style seems to be the guiding principle — although a maritime influence, as in the sharp-prowed Technium 2 building, is frequently discernible.

It's often difficult, in the early stages of a regeneration project, to attract new businesses to a building site, but the WDA, having made a priority of establishing the development's infrastructure, seem to have had little trouble in luring players such as the legal firm Morgan Cole to the banks of the Tawe, the first to establish an office here. There will be 65,000 square metres of business and office space to fill, along with 2000 flats and houses. When Bellway's Altamar apartments first went on the market such was the demand, before even a pile had been driven, that prospective buyers camped out for three days in the hope of bagging a flat, at prices ranging from £125,000 for a one-bedroom property to £195,000 for a two-bedroom.

The development is expected to generate demand for £40m's worth of goods and services from local business, and to create, eventually, thousands of jobs. It has already led to a doubling of house prices in the neighbouring community of St Thomas. Are, then, the people of St Thomas on the verge of being priced out of their locality — as many have been built out of their views across the bay by SA1's higher risers, the tallest of which will be 19 storeys high? Or might SA1 succeed in dissolving the old east/west divide, only for the eastside to develop its own internal, north/south divide, between working-class St Thomas, Danygraig and Port Tennant, north of Fabian Way, and the chic moneyed enclave south of that thoroughfare? I asked a couple of St Thomas lads fishing in the dock what their catch consisted of. "All sorts," said one, "but the fishing's not what it was, not since they started all... this," he sneered.

"You don't approve of SA1, then?"

"Certainly bloody don't. There was nothing wrong with Swansea before. Why'd they have to go and mess it up with all this? It's for rich people, innit? It'll just make more places for robbing and crime."

Like many Swansea people, I'm looking forward to drinking an espresso on the waterfront terraces of SA1, which seems likely to become the most appealing café quarter in the whole of Wales. SA1 may have become the city's trendiest address, but what may not be appreciated by many of those moving into its balconied duplexes is that they share a postcode with some of the poorest communities in Wales. It will take more than Swansea's long delayed saunter down the seaside path to cure the social ills of Bonymaen, Mayhill and Townhill, let alone those of similarly straitened communities beyond the confines of SA1.

PLANET 174

The Lower Swansea Valley

In this the first of two articles on historical industrial sites in Swansea, Nigel Jenkins considers the claim of the Lower Swansea Valley for World Heritage status.

Swansea wasted no time, when the opportunity arose in the 1960s, in obliterating all but a few traces of the industries which, over a 250-year period, had made it "Copperopolis", a world leader in the production of not only copper, but also steel, tinplate and zinc. A local authority which in 1957 had itched to demolish the town's medieval castle, and in 1960 had overseen the destruction of the Mumbles railway — which had been established in 1804 as a mineral line but which later became famous as the world's first passenger train — was clearly disinclined to take a conservationist view of any aspect of the post-industrial, poisoned moonscape that for decades had blighted the north-eastern approach to the town.

In its metallurgical heyday, the landscape of the Lower Swansea Valley had been one of the awe-inspiring wonders of the industrialising world. George Borrow (1803-81), touring "Wild Wales" in 1854, had stood transfixed by the "accursed pandemonium" of smoke, filth and fire which he observed from the valley side. "So strange a scene I had never beheld in nature," he wrote. "Had it been on canvas, with the addition of a number of diabolical figures... it might have stood for Sabbath in Hell... and would have formed a picture worthy of the powerful but insane painter Hieronymous Bosch." By the mid-twentieth century, when the abandonment of heavy industry in favour of service industries was well under way, this exhausted industrial landscape was spectacular still — for the extravagance of its devastation and the seeming impossibility of doing anything to make good one of the most polluted places on earth. A post-war "clean sweep" mentality, which had cheered on the rebuilding of the town centre after its destruction in the Blitz, combined with an urgent commitment, after the Aberfan disaster of 1966, to rid the post-industrial environment of its most degraded and dangerous features, and to reclaim derelict sites for new uses. Coal, copper, steel and tinplate may have been the making of old Swansea, but for many of those charged with the remaking of post-war Swansea, memories would have been all too raw of how their immediate forebears had lived lives, in those "satanic mills", of unremitting hardship. In their drive, to quote the poet Bryn Griffiths,

to erase the stain of the past,
to seed earth soured by a century
of slag and sulphur fumes,
to heal the cankered sore that
is today Landore

the authorities gave hardly a second, sentimental thought to certain structures within the wreckage which industrial archaeologists informed them were of major international importance. They called in the Territorial Army, during the 1960s, to raze to the ground half a dozen sites, paying little heed to pleas from the Royal Commission on Ancient Monuments to preserve selected, historically significant buildings.

Between 1960 and 1990, the Lower Swansea Valley was indeed transformed, especially the devastated valley bottom between the A48 Llansamlet-Morriston road in the north and the Hafod to the south — an area on the map looking like a stubby, upended bottle pointing towards the sea. Particularly striking, east of the Tawe, are extensive plantations of larch, pine, birch and alder on land that it was once assumed would never again support life of any kind. The region became renowned as a laboratory for pollution and reclamation scientists. Where there were huge boulders of fused slag, mounds of multi-coloured toxic waste, crumbling smokestacks, decaying smelter sheds and abandoned sidings, there's now an American-style enterprise "park", with banal rows of retail sheds, offices and car parks, together with light industrial and manufacturing units. Dotted among them are a couple of ponds, teeming with coarse fish, and the lawnfringed Fendrod Lake, dug out of the highly contaminated Fendrod marsh as a flood prevention measure, with its ducks and swans, picnic tables and fishing stages. If the dry ski slope and the Morfa athletics stadium have come and gone, there's no escaping the dazzling white, £30m Liberty Stadium at Landore, home of the Swans and the Ospreys since 2005. Looking like a multi-limbed, metal crab that could scuttle sideways at any moment, the stadium compels attention as the dominant structure in a landscape in which leisure and consumerism are now kings.

In spite of the insouciant haste with which the trappings of heavy industry were swept away, the Lower Swansea Valley nevertheless contains over twenty industrial sites of national and international importance — not that Swansea encourages any interest in them. It's possible to follow an industrial trail of sorts, but you have to find your own way, there being no readily available published guide. It's a landscape of superlatives, with traces at every turn of "the world's first this" and "the world's largest that", but unless you've read up on the area, you have next to no idea what you're looking at.

If Swansea seems not to want to know about its industrial past, there are those elsewhere for whom that renowned history is a magnet. It's a sweltering July morning in 2006, and I'm walking the valley with Dr Keir Reeves, a cultural historian from the University of Melbourne, who's touring key post-industrial sites in Europe, chief among them the china clay district of Cornwall, the world heritage site at Blaenafon — and Swansea. He's been commissioned by the Australian government to come up with ideas for the development of the former gold-mining region of Victoria as a world heritage environment. How do you conserve such landscapes? How do you encourage visitors? What interpretive facilities should be provided? How, in industrial, scientific and cultural terms, do you explain the significance of such andscapes and their residues? He's hoping that Swansea might help him towards some answers, while I'm thinking, the longer we walk and talk, that Keir might have some answers for Swansea.

I've warned him that as far as industrial remains are concerned there's not that much to see — although submerged beneath the retail sheds, the newer suburbs and the redistributed copper waste that was used to level off a chaotic landscape there are undoubtedly important structural and mechanical remains. Tramping along a tarmacked former railway line to the east of the Tawe, we can delight in the stretch of new forest that borders the path, but we also share a sense of regret at how the greening of parts of the valley has obliterated so much of the industrial heritage.

The banks of the river that ferried the copper ore — from Cornwall, Anglesey, Cuba, Chile and elsewhere — directly to the coal that was used to smelt it, are walkable only here and there. From the Quay Parade bridge near the docks, both banks look promising. But after about 300 metres, the west bank path comes to an abrupt halt at the fence that surrounds the massive black sheds of the pipe work engineering firm Unit Superheating. On this site, between 1764 and 1870, the Cambrian Pottery turned out its world famous Swansea china. A string of commercial and light industrial concerns, and thereafter housing in the Hafod, keep the western riverbank inaccessible for nearly a kilometre. The best bet is therefore the eastern path. Its riverside stretch, before it veers right to skirt the forestry, is dotted with Swansea Harbour Trust mooring bollards, reminders of the almost continuous wharves that once lined the river as far as Morriston; several of these quaysides are still intact.

The presiding genius of the western side of the valley — up ahead of us, on a crag overlooking Landore — is Morris "Castle", the ruined tenement block which John Morris I (1745-1819), the founder of Morriston, built for his colliers in the 1770s. It's said to be among the earliest examples of tenement-style living since Roman times. That of the eastern side, immediately to our right, is Kilvey Hill, which George Borrow described as "a lofty green mountain". It would not be green for much longer. The fumes belching from the industries below — some 2,325,000 cubic feet of sulphuric acid a day were being released into the air — soon poisoned its vegetation and turned its western flanks more or less black. In this morning's bright sunlight, Kilvey's underlying Pennant sandstone — the stone from which so much of Swansea was built — exposed by the odd (disused) quarry, gleams a rich dark gold, and higher up the 200-metre hill there are one or two smallholdings with paddocks, jumps and horses.

The first major industrial site we come to is that of the White Rock Copperworks (1737-1929), cleared by the Territorial Army in the early 1960s, but designated the White Rock Industrial Archaeology Park in the 1980s when significant remains were excavated and consolidated. It was the first copper smelter to be built on the east bank of the river and the third of what would eventually total eleven riverside copper-works. Its most obvious feature is a spiral path inscribed playfully on a broad grassy mound. This is all that remains of a monstrous spoil tip, the bulk of which — 183,000 tons of it — was dumped on the site of the Upper Forest and Worcester tinplate works four kilometres away at Morriston, where it formed a platform above the flood-plain of the Tawe for the construction of the Morganite Carbon factory. Other notable features include part of the Pennant sandstone smelting hall known as "The Great Workhouse", a cut-and-cover canal tunnel, sandstone quays, and a re-excavated and beautifully conserved seventeenth-century river dock — perhaps the most evocative remnant of all. Forget the overgrown greensward underfoot and the thick foliage on either side of the river, and imagine the Tawe confounded again with flame and industrial ferment, and a laden Cape Horner — thrusting bowsprit, towering masts — looming majestically through the noxious smokes billowing from all sides, her local crew thronging the deck, desperate to get ashore after six to nine months at sea. If Swansea had a more visionary attitude towards its industrial and maritime heritage, there might be ambitious plans for the reconstruction of one of its famous copperore barques, such as the *Zeta* (1865), after which the most-beautiful-Welshwoman-in-Hollywood was named.

What goods were made from the ore the Cape Horners brought home? Copper sheathing for the hulls of timber ships (hence that term of assurance "copper bottomed"), bolts, hinges, glazing bars, roofing material, coins, harness parts, buttons, buckles, toys, kitchen utensils, boilers, pipes, vats, rollers, wires, plates. Many of these things were manufactured in centres such as Birmingham, Bristol, Liverpool and London, after Swansea had produced the raw material in the form of fine copper ingots. Swansea copper also played a shameful role in the slave-dependent economies of the eighteenth and nineteenth centuries. Various Swansea smelters produced copper "rods" and horse-shoe shaped "manillas" for bartering for slaves in Africa, White Rock being an early producer of manillas.

Directly opposite the White Rock site, and all but lost in a jungle of buddleia, birch and ivy, is the saw-toothed roof of the Vivian company's loco shed, built to house Britain's first ever standard-gauge articulated locomotive. Deciding on a closer examination, we cross the river via the A4217 road bridge, taking stock as we go of the wider human environment: Morriston to the north —

dominated by the ornate steeple of Tabernacl — the first and largest of the settlements founded by the coppermasters; the terraces to the east built for their workers by the Grenfell family and known as Grenfelltown (it's now Pentrechwyth); the self-contained copperworkers' community of the Hafod to the immediate west, founded by the copper magnate John Henry Vivian and known initially as Trevivian or Vivianstown; the terraces of Brynhyfryd, Landore and Plasmarl, and the huge chapels of quintessentially Welsh design — Siloh Newydd, Dinas Noddfa — scattered domineeringly among them.

"This is one hell of a landscape," says Keir. "I was expecting something, sure, but nothing as fascinating as this."

What he finds difficult to understand is why Swansea appears so reluctant to celebrate its unique industrial heritage and why the few internationally significant structures that remain are so shamefully neglected, as if being willed to destruction by the elements, vandalism and time.

The most prominent industrial relics on the valley bottom, which we pass en route to the loco shed, are proclaimed by their smokestacks: two engine houses belonging to the Vivian's Hafod Works (1810-1924), which by 1842 was the largest copperworks in the world. Built in the early 1860s and 1910 respectively, these roofless, rotting structures are supposedly secured against vandals by a spiked fence, some of which has been cut away to provide relatively easy access for the graffiti artists who have evidently been at work on their walls. Fenced doubly securely within the fence is some rolling machinery, clearly so "valuable" that, for years, it's been exposed on all sides to the weather. Uphill from the engine houses is the Landore Social Club, which used to be the works office. Opposite the club is a chunky sandstone structure, a rare survivor of the 54 limekilns once dotted along the Swansea Canal, for burning Mumbles limestone.

The loco shed is unfenced, other than by the almost impenetrable buddleia. You can just make out through the foliage large letters in white brickwork, along its eastern wall, spelling out "V & S [i.e. Vivian and Son] Ltd No. 1 SHED". The shed is built chiefly of the Vivian company's light grey, slag-based "patent" brick, which tends, in time, to crumble. The somewhat spayed walls are mostly intact, but the shattered roof is dangerously unstable. Without urgent attention, the collapse of this important building will surely be complete in a year or two.

The graffitists have been up to their expert, if garish, labours along a riverside wall nearby, and they have managed to get inside some robustly fenced remains of the historic Morfa Works (1835-1980), just round the corner at the Landore park-and-ride. Distinguished by its skeletal clock turret and the exposed timbers of its roof, charred after a recent fire and close to caving in, this late nineteenth-century, Grade II listed building was the works' electrical powerhouse before becoming the canteen building of Yorkshire Imperial Metals, the last owners of the combined Hafod and Morfa works. Nearby is an old rolling mill shed, now used by Swansea Museum as a store, which at the time of its construction in the 1840s was the largest of its kind in the world.

We continue upriver on the west side of the Tawe. On the opposite bank, incorporated into the huge Addis plastics factory, are three reroofed smelting halls (c.1838-42) of the old Upper Bank Works (1757), in which the first ever Mutz Yellow Metal was made for the sheathing of ships' hulls. With their characteristic ventilated gable ends and the foundations of furnaces under their floors, these Grade II listed structures are the last roofed smelting halls in Swansea. The whole site has been earmarked for residential development — Barratt Homes' £100m, 550-unit Copper Quarter scheme — and conservationists have been campaigning to save the sheds from demolition. The council eventually decided to permit demolition of two of them, but to insist on the retention of the best preserved as a "landmark" building in the new (and necessarily well-heeled) "community", enisled by whizzing traffic and the out-of-town shopping sheds you find all over Britain: Sports World, TK Maxx, Morrisons, Pizza Hut, Next, George.

Another gently decaying Grade II structure nearby is the remarkable iron and timber bascule bridge (1919), over which slag was transported from the Morfa works to tips on the east side of the Tawe. By means of hydraulic power — the filling of a water tank at its western end — its deck would tilt upwards, to allow sailing ships to pass along the river.

The path continues alongside the Liberty Stadium and between the towering stone piers of Brunel's magnificent Landore Viaduct (1847-50), most of which was built originally of timber. This bridge too was designed to give clearance to sailing ships.

It was on a site just south of the viaduct that, in the 1860s, William Siemens perfected the open-hearth process that revolutionised the production of steel. Nothing now remains of the Landore Siemens Steel Company buildings. Nor is there any trace, just north of the viaduct, of the earliest copper-smelting works in the valley, the Llangyfelach Copperworks (1717).

We carry on towards Morriston, switching — over a new footbridge at Plasmarl — to the east bank. Here, on a triangular plot in the lee of Makro, is the Pantyblawd Road site of the only statutory "gipsy' encampment in the county. The gipsies, or travellers as they call themselves, have long been part of the valley scene, and have frequently suffered persecution. Any "trouble" in valley communities is usually perceived to be the doing of "rough" elements from elsewhere in the valley, with the "gipsies" often — and unfairly — getting the blame.

On the outskirts of Morriston, we turn back towards town, taking a detour through the Hafod, currently undergoing a major programme of renovation. The re-rendering of many of the terraces of what is the best conserved copperworkers' township in Swansea is startlingly attractive.

By the end of our tour, Keir is astonished that, in spite of the late twentieth-century "obliterations", so much survives of the industrial whirlwind that made Swansea's name — from the remains of works and transportation systems, to the communities built for the workers and some of the mansions the magnates built for themselves in Swansea west (where there is also the exceptionally well "fossilised" industrial landscape of Clyne Valley). "If anywhere in Wales deserves world heritage status it's Swansea," he says. "Swansea should go for it. It ticks just about every world heritage box."

With worries about a projected bill of £30m to renovate the Guildhall, and about further millions to repair the Grand Theatre and extend the Glynn Vivian Art Gallery (to say nothing of the dismaying poverty suffered by thousands of the city's inhabitants), the conservation and promotion of Swansea's industrial heritage is obviously way beyond Swansea's financial capabilities. Without the international recognition (and funds) that would flow from achieving something like world heritage status, it seems inevitable that the neglect and deterioration will continue. Whether Swansea has the vision to pursue such an ambition — which might represent in the longer term a more creative opportunity for the city than the current obsession with building flashy waterside apartments for the rich — must, sadly, remain in doubt.

PLANET 181

Hidden Heritage: Clyne Valley

*The second of two articles on Swansea's unique but
neglected industrial landscape*

Carved out by the violence of colossal meltwater torrents at the end
of the last ice age, Clyne Valley, with its extensive tracts of woodland
either side of a meandering stream, would seem today to represent
the essence of pastoral quietude. Few who visit the Clyne Valley
Country Park stray much from the foot and bike path laid down on
the trackbed of the old LMS line, which, until its closure in 1964,
carried Swansea-Shrewsbury trains over the Mumbles road at
Blackpill, at the park's southern edge, and on through Killay, 2.5
kilometres away at its northern boundary. But in among the trees
you will find, if you know where to look, a fossilised industrial
landscape, unsuspected by most locals, which is in a much fuller
state of preservation than the more famous industrial environment
of the Lower Swansea Valley.

Cut along the line of demarcation between the Lower and Middle
Coal Measures, the valley was a crucible of industrial activity until
well into the twentieth century, with — at various times — coal and
iron mines, bell pits, quarries, canals, railways, cart tracks, leets (for
water power), brickworks, iron and copper smelters, an arsenic
works and wood-based industries for the production of charcoal,
naptha and cellulose. Evidence of many of these undertakings is still
to be found, but the search for such traces is hampered in places by
an almost impenetrable undergrowth of wildly out of control
rhododendron of the pestilential *Ponticum ponticum* variety.

The rhododendron problem, I discover on a walk through the
park one spring afternoon in 2006, is being addressed on an
industrial scale. With my *compañera* the jazz singer Margot Morgan,

I head up Mill Lane, Blackpill, and enter the forest opposite Clyne Castle — one of several Swansea-west piles that belonged to the Vivian coppermaster dynasty, and which is now being converted into luxury apartments — to follow a route along the valley's western rim. Huge machines with man-high wheels are parked here for the weekend, the mud motorway they've carved — to get at the rhododendrons — stretching northwards through the trees. We take, initially, a smaller track forking left and soon come to what looks like a castellated medieval tower. This was built as an exhaust stack for noxious fumes from the arsenic works a couple of hundred metres down the slope. In the 1860s, it was turned into a Gothic pavilion, and named the Ivy Tower, by William Graham Vivian of Clyne Castle. Looking for the arsenic works, we head directly downhill, crossing the mud thoroughfare, and follow, through the dead leaves and wispy undergrowth, a line of irregular holes — which are caved-in portions of the tunnel that connected the tower to the works.

The works' ivy-clad ruins are indeed substantial: the stump of another stack with a sawn off tree-trunk sticking out of its stonework, the remains of furnaces encrusted with crystallised arsenic, flue labyrinths, an office block with fireplaces, windows, doorways and rotting lintels, lengths of wall as high in places as six or nine metres. Built in the mid 1840s from Pennant sandstone rubble quarried nearby, the Clyne Wood Arsenic Works fell into disuse about fifteen years later, probably because of its proximity to the country mansions of members of the powerful Morris and Vivian dynasties, who could tolerate a few coal mines in the valley beneath them but not the highly poisonous arsenic fumes that were gusting from those stacks. That so much of the works has survived into the present is due partly to its subsequent re-use as hay sheds and partly to the dense foliage on the slope around it, which has rendered it largely invisible and relatively inaccessible. As "The only eighteenth-century or early nineteenthcentury works in the former world centre of the non-ferrous smelting industry to preserve remains of its productive plant" — to quote John Newman — it's an important site; but Swansea, as usual, couldn't seem to care less.

We return to the muddy high road, the woodland on either side of which has been so thoroughly unclogged of rhododendron that many old field boundaries, from before the forestation of the area, are visible in the form of shallow mossy banks. The track, with great wheelrutted offshoots, sometimes passes between huge banks of rhododendron trunks and branches bound together like giant *fasces*, awaiting removal. On reaching a clearing where bluebells have pushed up through the cindered remains of recently burned vegetation, we hear a loud metallic banging — and head towards the source of the sound. We find a couple of lads with spades and a wheelbarrow working away at some earthy troughs and humps. They look like students on an archaeological dig. I ask them what they're investigating. They're reluctant to be drawn, but Margot gets them to admit that they're building a series of ramps for their mountain bikes. In a few weeks time, when the ferns have grown back, their switchback should be well hidden from prying eyes.

With verdant farmland to our left and, to our right, views over Swansea as far as the mountains beyond Neath, we press on past the isolated Keeper's Cottage (designed, like so many of the estate's buildings, by Graham Vivian, "without benefit of architect"), and begin to descend through the bushes, passing another cindered expanse, mostly of singed birches, which is criss-crossed with old cart tracks. Here the bike boys have constructed yet more switchbacks. A cart track, which soon becomes a metre- deep holloway, leads us — via more daredevil ramps, some designed to propel a bike clean across the defile — steeply downhill past the remains of a number of bell pits. Identifiable as mounds of waste on the lower side of shallow, basin-shaped sinks, sometimes waterfilled, bell pits were primitive coal workings formed by miners digging a hole a little over a metre in diameter and three metres deep, then belling out at the bottom as far as they dared, without bringing the roof down on top of them. There are scores of them dotted around the valley, particularly on the western side of the bike path after about the half-way point between Blackpill and Killay.

Not far from the valley bottom — we can hear the stream below us — we come to the most dramatic of Clyne's coal-mine sites, the collapsed mine-shaft of the Coed yr Ysgol colliery; the remaining conical pit is clearly much in use these days by the bike boys as a sort of plunge of death. Tall, thin trees are well established on the spoil tips round about, and sticking out of the undergrowth is an abandoned steam-powered engine which once hauled trams from an inclined entrance tunnel. A plaque on this rusting hulk reads "J Wild and Co Ltd Oldham/1891".

Deciding on a pint roughly half way through our walk, we cross the stream, scramble up the embankment and head along the bike path towards the Railway Inn at Killay, about half a kilometre up the line, passing under a sturdy bridge, at eit her end of which lurks a Second World War pillbox. Strung out alongside the path, for most of the distance, are hundreds of metres of video tape.

The Railway, perched alongside the platform of the old station, is a proper pub: no 24-hour wide-screen inanities; no "gastropub" pretensions; no conversation-zapping jukebox or muzak — but congenial locals and welcoming bar staff, a choice of three rooms to drink in (or an outside terrace), and quite simply the best beer in the world, Original Wood. It's available at only one other outlet, the Joiner's at Bishopston, where this nectar of the Celtic deities is brewed. That the Railway has survived the homogenising, profit-crazy mania that has destroyed so many pubs is a wonder — attributable, says the landlord, to two things: the beer from the Joiner's and the fact that the pub is council — rather than brewery

— owned (and leased out on a monthly basis).

Savouring our Woods at a table outside, we wonder about that video tape. Easier by far, given the right equipment, to recover those images scattered and scrunched up along the bike path than to recall anything at all of the lives of the hundreds who toiled away their short lives in this valley — until well within "living memory", as they say... except that "living memory" seems to have forgotten everything about them. The homes they lived in, the food they ate, the joys and pains of their relationships, their exhausting labours, the diseases and accidents they suffered and died from. Gone, utterly; vanished as surely as the last puff of steam from that old engine in the woods. Once in a rare while, an historian or a poet will attempt to raise a voice for them. In "An Old Lie Out", for instance, the Swansea poet John Beynon commemorates the miners who were drowned when the sea broke into colliery workings under Swansea Bay. The owners, denying that certain men had lost their lives, refused their families compensation. But years later, a high tide caused the water level to rise up the old shaft in Clyne Valley, and the skeletal miners, as the poem has them declare, "were spat out, one by one,/The rank earth repelling all their lies/And our voiceless anger gloriously sown."

The distorted seams of the "South Crop" of the coalfield made it increasingly difficult — and unprofitable — to mine coal in Clyne, and the last of the valley's mines closed in the 1920s, leaving brick-making as Clyne's sole industry. We drain our glasses, head back down the bike path and, soon after the bridge-with-pillboxes, veer left through the trees along the raised track of a former tramway leading to Rhyd-y-defaid colliery. The red brick road, we call the track, after the hundreds of locally made bricks embedded in its surface. We soon come to a tree-shaded pond and the site of the last of Clyne's brickworks which, shortly before it closed in the 1950s, was producing 75,000 bricks a week. There are no buildings to be seen, but there are a couple of mounds of thousands of warped, bulbous, doubled, broken or otherwise misshapen bricks which have been rejected. They're stamped variously "Evans-Bevan Ltd/Clyne Works/Killay", "Clyne/Killay" or simply "Killay". I slip one into my knapsack for a doorstop.

The embanked tramway, passing straight as a Roman road through the trees, takes us to the Rhyd-y-defaid colliery site, where there's another pond, some fragments of wall, and extensive, wooded spoilheaps. We turn right, on the main path from Killay to Sketty, in the direction of Olchfa Wood, hoping to find some sign of the racecourse, complete with grandstand, that was established in fields around here in the nineteenth century. Although it was Swansea's prime racecourse by the 1920s, all seems to have been obliterated — either by dense, brambly undergrowth or by the huge (and hugely controversial) municipal tip that sprawled northwards for over a kilometre, from Ynys Newydd Road in Lower Sketty, during the 1970s and 1980s. The proximity of this tip, with its rats, flies and foul odours, to Derwen Fawr, one of the most "select" areas of Swansea, always seemed a little curious. To the denizens of "Dehn Vah", as many of them mispronounce the place, the dump was an affront and they campaigned vociferously against it, forcing its closure in the mid 1980s.

Anyone who remembers the gargantuan quantities of waste that were dumped here during those decades — and the noisy, fume-belching drama (beneath a constant cloud of scavenging gulls) of bulldozers, earth removers and huge tractors with iron-spiked wheels — would be surprised at the transformation of the dump into a bosky plateau, several metres high, of reeds, rushes, gorse, hawthorn, blackthorn, pussy willow, primroses and vast, impenetrable tracts of bramble. The plateau stops a few metres short of the once handsome but now ruined New Mill Farm and extends south, between the stream and Mill Wood, to a still busy collection point for garden refuse, dead furniture and defunct white goods, which are then removed in giant containers. The depot's a hive of activity at weekends.

The contents of the plateau seem well disguised until, here and there, a path gives way to a muddy puddle, through which protrude broken bottles, squashed cans and plastic bags. The tip itself has hidden forever both the site of Sir John Morris's Ynys Collieries (after which Ynys Newydd Road is named) and that of the Clyne Valley Colliery, which closed in the early 1920s. What became the Mumbles railway could be said to have started here, for it was to the Ynys Collieries initially, rather than to Oystermouth, that the Oystermouth Railway was destined, first and foremost as a mineral line. Laid down in 1804, it curved sharply northwards from what is now Mumbles Road and followed a line taking it 100 metres up the present Derwen Fawr Road; it passed along the lane that gives access these days to a scattering of secluded houses — CCTV protected, spiky gates, stockade fencing, "guard dogs loose" — on the eastern side of the stream, before veering away in the direction of the mines. Some sleepers were still visible in the 1970s, but the tip eventually obliterated the track into the colliery. The left side of the lane, as we head downstream towards Blackpill, is still banked and walled by the railway's high-quality stonework. Among dead leaves on the bank we find a contorted length of abandoned rail.

Back at Blackpill, the scene today — apart from the relentlessly busy Mumbles road — seems tranquil: two men fishing with a drag net at the mouth of the river; beach artists making transient sculptures out of sand, driftwood, feathers, shells; young families splashing about at the lido. It's known, inevitably, as the gateway to Gower. But Blackpill was once a hub of industry, with coal being shipped from the sands and, later, from a quay on the foreshore, which has since disappeared. The area could have developed like a small-scale Lower Swansea Valley, had a consortium of industrialists pursued a plan to build furnaces on the banks of the pill. But the project fell through and the local coal mines were worked out by the 1920s, by which time Blackpill had settled into the role of country estate village, as nature reclaimed the remarkable industrial landscape of Clyne.

PLANET 182

References: Ralph A. Griffiths (ed.), *The City of Swansea: Challenges and Change* (Sutton, 1990); Stephen Hughes, *Copperopolis, Landscapes of the Early Industrial Period in Swansea* (Royal Commission on the Ancient and Historical Monuments of Wales, 2000); John Newman, *The Buildings of Wales: Glamorgan* (Penguin, 1995); Glanmor Williams (ed.), *Swansea, an Illustrated History* (Christopher Davies, 1990).

The Old Central Library

Nigel Jenkins on Shelf Life, *a collaboration between
National Theatre Wales, Volcano Theatre and Welsh
National Opera set in Swansea's Old Library*

Wales, at long last, has an English-medium national theatre, which seems, this time, to be more than some thespian's short-lived pipedream. It's a balmy evening in early April 2010, after the coldest winter in thirty years, and I'm milling around in the courtyard between the old police station and the old central library, sipping a glass of wine which came "free" with a very expensive packet of crisps, contemplating a mountain of discarded books, and waiting for the second of National Theatre Wales's twelve inaugural productions, *Shelf Life*, to spark into action. The show's an unlikely collaboration between John E. McGrath's NTW, Welsh National Opera and Swansea's own tirelessly experimental, and internationally renowned, Volcano theatre company — all stitched together by directors Paul Davies and Catherine Bennett, and dramaturg D.J. Britton — which, we are soon to find, works admirably.

Volcano, who often like to stage their extravaganzas in numinous buildings, have not been alone in falling for the charms of the old library, with its captivating domed reading room reminiscent, in miniature, of the British Museum's. It was the ideal setting for the 1962 film *Only Two Can Play*, which was adapted from Kingsley Amis's novel *That Uncertain Feeling* (1955). It starred Peter Sellers as a feckless librarian and laughably ineffectual lecher, while Kenneth Griffith, playing his colleague, turned in a memorable performance as an emotionally constipated, henpecked husband.

Since the old library was emptied of its books in 2007 and its functions transferred to the new central library in the Civic Centre on the seafront, it has been in the care of the Welsh School of Architectural Glass, who are not quite sure what to do with it. But filmmakers, including the makers of *Dr Who*, have been queuing up to use the circular reading room, and it's a lull in filmic proceedings that gives Volcano and Co. a three-week run of this faded beauty of a building.

For 120 years, it served as a storehouse of knowledge. Fact and fiction, gossip and wisdom — it was all collected here. Volcano are interested not only in the narratives and information gathered in the books, but in the stories accumulated by the building itself. What does it mean to close a library? What have libraries been in the past and what might they become? What future for the book in this relentlessly digitising age?

Swansea's first public library opened in Goat Street (roughly commensurate with what is today upper Princess Way) in 1871. It was far too small from the outset, and was replaced by the Central Library and School of Art in 1887, built in Italian-classical style on land which previously housed "dens of debauchery and obscenity", to quote a local magistrate. It was clearly meant to exert a significant improving influence on the moral and intellectual life of the town, although not all members of Swansea's upper echelons were in favour. The Morriston colliery owner John Glasbrook, who had successfully delayed the founding of a free library, had claimed in 1870 that "people have too much knowledge already; it was much easier to manage them twenty years ago; the more education people get the more difficult they are to manage."

A contrary view was expressed by the former (and future) prime minister William Gladstone who, invited to open the Central Library on 6 June 1887, declared that "Without the blessings of reading, the burden of life would be intolerable." A small bust of the Liberal leader used to be kept in the reading room; it's been replaced tonight by a theatrically large portrait of Gladstone, which, after being paraded through the courtyard on a ceremonial litter, is ensconced in the reading room, to preside over the proceedings with a bemused eye.

With audience numbers limited to only thirty per performance, *Shelf Life*'s two performances a night are sell-outs. While we wait for the litter, the actors and the WNO's community choir to sweep into the courtyard, a lone performer beneath a tasselled pagoda wipes old hardbacks with a wet cloth, dilating whimsically on the glory of books. As daylight turns to dusk, I notice how the sky, contaminated by dust from that Icelandic volcano, has turned an extraordinary green. Celebs in this evening's audience include Michael Sheen, the Hollywood star from Port Talbot, and the poet Owen Sheers, who are no doubt picking up some ideas for a future NTW collaborative project, namely a re-telling of the Port Talbot passion play which used to be performed annually in Margam Park until the mid 1990s. As the book-wiper's eulogy peaks, she plunges the volume into her washing-up bowl, and into the courtyard irrupts the cast, with the choir in full voice, modestly attired to look like librarians, but sporting here and there Dionysian masks.

This tension between measured decorum and sensory abandon — sex in the stacks, nudity among the desks — is an insistent, alluring undertow throughout the evening. As the choir sing about libraries, an aerial dancer suspended on a rope from the rim of the reference library's roof twirls as she swings in ever wider arcs, jotting notes on scraps of paper and, with growing effort, pinning them on increasingly far flung parts of the drum's stone wall. Between songs, there are snatches of drama, as when a Nordic blonde pursues a young man with a rolled up newspaper, beating out of him an admission of sexual "infidelity".

We are then invited into the stacks, at ground-floor level beneath the library. Bathed in red light, these narrow, brick corridors of book-bereft, wooden shelving remind the woman in front me of the Roman catacombs. Fragments of stacking instructions are pinned here and there:

WELSH POOL
Authors with bardic or literary titles filed under family surname
"Ceiriog" = Hughes, J. Ceiriog
"Crwys" = Williams, M. Crwys
"Gwenallt" = Jones, D. "Gwenallt"
"Emrys ap Iwan" = Jones, Robert Ambrose

And there are intriguing snippets of graffiti to be stumbled on, some perhaps original, some almost certainly "Volcani": "Bong on"; "Librarians make novel lovers"; "GOM = God's Only Mistake" (which is what Gladstone's detractors called the "Grand Old Man"); "Kardomah Gang's hideout was razed to the snow — DT"; "Today is not what it should be."

Here again, in a cosy alcove, is the book-washing one, still waxing lyrical about literature, while whisking up in a measuring jug milk, eggs (with shell) and cinnamon, before decanting the brew into a mug and drinking it. She's going out shortly, she says, and would we like to accompany her while she puts on her make-up? She leads us into a nearby section where there are five life-size posters of the *Shelf Life* actors, naked. This would seem to refer to the story — which I have yet to find reliably authenticated — that following the Three Nights Blitz of 1941 the stacks were used as a mortuary for some of those killed in the bombardment. (Later, it's said that although the books smelled of burned flesh for years afterwards, people continued to borrow them. Is this more Volcanic ash? What to take literally and what not, from these mythic remembrancers?). Chatting as she applies her make-up, the player asks what we think of her lipstick — Paviland Ochre. Only Phil George of the BBC and

I seem to get this gigglesome aside.[1]

We are then directed up some steps, at the top of which the Nordic blonde is skipping vigorously, reeling off all her dreams and ambitions — before halting abruptly, to declare that she's fulfilled not one of them. Then, in return for, say, a hug or a swivel of a customer's hips, she gives each of us what seems to be a genuine, individually numbered reader's ticket — "Swansea Library/ Alexandra Road/Books may not be taken/out of the library" — before ushering us into the magnificent reading room, where a central round table is piled high with cheeses, grapes, olives and loaves of bread, and candlelight gleams on silverware and glasses.

The idea here, explains the company, is that "We have imagined one last meeting of the custodians of the library — ghosts or angels, or mortals like us, opinions, arguments, vanities and hopes: the old library hears them all and it trusts that you, our readers, will enjoy the experience..."

As we wait for the rest of the audience to emerge from the stacks, we're invited to help ourselves to grapes and wander round, sampling information about libraries printed on large posters hanging over empty shelves. With most of the books and reading desks removed, the relative silence here is of a different kind from the intensely busy quiet of the reading room's heyday, when all manner of researchers — self-improving dockers, political activists, professors from the university — would be found here side by side, immersed in reading and note-taking. Built at a time of enlightenment, the rigidities of the class system were nevertheless inscribed in the building, with an entrance at the rear for the lower orders, while "polite society" entered at the front. A paternalist care for the people's moral wellbeing was reflected in various acts of censorship. In 1899, for instance, it was decided that the racing tips in daily newspapers should be blacked out. Rules and regulations in the early days included: no animals, no smoking, no spitting, no eating, no talking, no tracing pictures, no striking matches, no children under 14 except with the librarian's permission; and anyone found selling or pawning a library book would be liable to prosecution for larceny.

Our numbered tickets entitle us to a free book each, which we retrieve by climbing the stairs to the balcony. No. 21 gets me Bill Bryson's *Short History of Nearly Everything*. An acquaintance with a restless love life gets *The Kama Sutra*.

Then the "final meeting" begins, as we descend from the balcony to take our seats facing the round table, around which the six players — who, by now, have become our friends — loosely gather to eat, drink, reminisce, philosophise, shout, murmur and kiss. From time to time, one or other of them peels away: to clamber up the wrought-iron supports of the balcony, for instance, or to stand on a column of books to recite a Tony Curtis poem about Singleton Hospital. They film each other with a hand-held camera, the images being shown on makeshift screens. During a somewhat worthy peroration delivered to us by an actor with his back to the others, the Nordic blonde and a cheeky young beardie gradually strip naked, freezing in a seated, reading position whenever the orator turns towards them. Although the actors are evidently under orders to frustrate both narrative and extended, coherent dialogue — by refusing to respond or react to each others' statements — the "meeting" nevertheless delivers many funny, provocative, wistful vignettes. The most moving is a hesitant and bashful recollection of a first love, communicated in evasive, fragmented, incomplete words and phrases: I've rarely heard such fumbling inarticulacy express, with stunning definition, such a depth of feeling.

It's dark enough, by now, for eidetic images of Swansea street scenes to be projected onto the glass of the dome itself, and it's time, alas, for the party to end.

A week or two later, I return to the scene. No round table.

Everything back to what looks like normal. But it isn't, quite. Gladstone's still there, and the colourful star in the middle of the floor, which the table had partly occluded, is not the library's original design: it's a legacy from *Dr Who*. And the books that once again fill the library's shelves are not books at all, but a sleight of theatrical hand... awaiting, any day now, the return of the Time Lord.

PLANET 200

---

1. For some of the show's references you had to be in the local know. It was in a cave at Paviland, Gower, in 1823, that the (then) earliest human bone finds in these islands were made. Some fossilised human bones stained with red ochre (or okra, as our actor pronounced it) were unearthed by Dean William Buckland, who wrongly concluded both that they were the bones of a young woman and that they were about 2000 years old. "The Red Lady of Paviland" turned out to be a young man from nearly 30,000 years ago.

Doing the Swansea Shuffle

Nigel Jenkins on the Swansea roots of
rhythm-and-bluesman Spencer Davis

It could be, in Swansea terms, an old rock star's definition of the blues: having nowhere to keep a pint of milk cool in the sweltering Tawe Delta heatwave of July 2006. Not only is Spencer "Keep on Running" Davis bereft of a fridge, he doesn't have a washing machine or anything else much in the house he has inherited from his mother in Mulberry Avenue, West Cross, and in which he finds himself more or less camping with a few sticks of furniture. Following her death three years ago, there was a somewhat "uneven" (and acrimonious) division of the spoils, which resulted in the house being divested, in his absence, of all that was moveable and saleable — which is why we are meeting at 8.00 a.m. at the Bay Wash Laundromat on the seafront at West Cross: he wants his wheelie-bag's worth of dirty washing done in time for a gig in Germany the day after tomorrow. In the meantime, he has arrangements to make at the Grand Theatre about a charity performance there in October for Macmillan Cancer Support (both his parents died of cancer), and he has kindly agreed to walk and talk me through the working-class community of Bonymaen, in north-east Swansea, where he was brought up.

Spencer Davis (b. 1939; the "e" was dropped as the result of a spelling mistake on the pressing of his first single) moved to the United States in 1970 and lives these days on Catalina Island (about forty kilometres south-west of Los Angeles), in the seaside town of Avalon which, he says, is rather like Swansea and whose name the locals mistakenly believe to be Spanish in origin; the Welshman knows better. Since the first rush of fame in the 1960s, with major hits such as "Keep on Running", "Somebody Help Me", "Gimme Some Lovin'" and "I'm a Man", he has toured almost constantly. By the end of this year (2006), he will have played more than 70 gigs in countries such as Holland, Belgium, Denmark, England, Trinidad, the United States, Wales, Australia and, above all, Germany, where audiences delight in his fluent command of their language.

But no matter how packed his schedule, he has not forgotten his Welsh roots (he's a supporter and honorary member of Plaid Cymru) and he has always found time for Swansea; he probably manages to spend as much time here as Bonnie Tyler, his rock-star near neighbour in West Cross, who has a palatial establishment near the sea's edge (as well as a house in Portugal). His mother's death at the age of 89, far from proposing any severance of the Swansea connection, seems to have reaffirmed his commitment to the area, in both practical and artistic terms. He's keeping on the former council house in Mulberry Avenue, having converted the loft into a spacious studio with a superb view over Swansea Bay, and he has campaigned on a number of local urban environment issues. His recently released 12-track album *So Far* marks a new departure, in that his writing has taken a distinctly autobiographical turn, with the home patch featuring on many of the songs: when he's not gigging "From door to door, coast to coast/Shakin' more hands than a talk-show host" we find him "Down in Wind Street on a Saturday night/When the glass is full and the moon is bright/Doing the Swansea shuffle."

The laundry deposited, we taxi up to Bonymaen, the dense traffic on Mumbles Road being a reminder of that folly of Swansea follies, the destruction, in 1960, of the Mumbles railway. "If they'd kept the Mumbles train, it would have contributed hugely to relieving the pressure of all this traffic," says Spencer, who pays fond homage on the new album to that "rockin' and a-rollin'" train to paradise. "With the new development in SA1 they're surely going to have to introduce a light railway — maybe from Port Talbot to Mumbles."

On the crawl through the car-clogged city centre we talk of his beginnings. He was born in Mountpleasant, at 71 North Hill Road. The family later lived at 13 Norfolk Street, which was destroyed in a bombing raid shortly after they'd left for Birkenhead and other towns in England, his father being in the army during the war. He was five when the family returned to Swansea and, eventually, a new home in Bonymaen. At Dynevor Boys School in the city centre — alma mater of other Swansea achievers such as Harry Secombe, Rowan Williams and Bernard Knight — he studied German, French and Spanish, and also did well at chemistry and English literature. "The music master was a man called Weber who, with Dewi Johns, the physics master, took great delight in physical punishment. Weber told me, 'you will never do anything in music.'"

Music, nevertheless, had him in its thrall from the moment in early childhood when his Uncle Herman called round with his mandolin. "Time stood still and the sun shone bright/On that dark and stormy night," Spencer sings on the jaunty, folk-inflected "Uncle Herman's Mandolin". The "far-off lands and sights" of which his uncle sang sent young Spencer travelling too — on a journey that has never ended. Later, someone gave him a harmonica: "I never put it down from the moment I got it." He asked his parents for a guitar for Christmas, "but they gave me a piano accordion. Hardly the same thing. But I managed to pick up a few carol tunes and I went round Bonymaen, aged about 11 or 12, making enough money to buy shoes and trousers, which gave me the taste for being a professional musician." Four or five years later, he got his first guitar and was soon playing American country music and blues with art college students and others. He performed regularly at venues such as the King's Arms in High Street and Rob's (all-night) Café in St Helen's Road. "I was playing with a harmonica bracket around my neck before I'd ever heard of Bob Dylan." The blues has remained a seminal influence: "Hooker and Leadbelly taught me how to be a man," he sings on a country-blues homage to the music that shaped his life.

Like many Welsh artists, he received unstinting support from his mother Mary, lovingly elegised on *So Far* as "My source of inspiration, tenderness and strength". "But my father," says Spencer, "was a dick-head. He abused me physically and, unable to stand the beatings any longer, in 1956, at the age of 16, I got out." Eighteen months as a civil servant in London — "in a paper prison of my own design" — proved not the escape he could have desired, and "I nearly lost all hope/Till Elvis, Fats and Buddy/They tossed me a rope". Refusing a stint of national service "fighting for the Queen", he returned to Swansea, completed his sixth-form education, went to Birmingham University in 1960 and eventually embarked on a teaching career that proved incompatible with his musical ambitions. "You're falling asleep, sir," his pupils observed one Monday morning after a hard weekend's gigging with the band. So he gave up the day job; the Rhythm and Blues Quartet he'd formed in 1963 with Pete Yorke and the Winwood brothers became the Spencer Davis Group — and the story thereafter is known the world over.

"The land beyond Jordan" is how early nineteenth-century Swansea society used to characterise the bleak and god-forsaken Bonymaen area (as it was perceived), with its cockfighting, boozing and womanising. The cockfighting may have fallen out of fashion, but Bonymaen, in common with similarly straitened communities such as Townhill and Blaenymaes, still has something of a "reputation" — undeserved, locals insist — thanks to headlines that accentuate the antics of a minority (car theft, joy-riding, racism, badger bashing) while taking little account of the palpable warmth, good humour and resourcefulness of the majority.

After an extended tea stop at the family home, in Jersey Road, of

Spencer's agent, Helen Clarke-Woods, we head off, with her uncle and Spencer's childhood friend Keith Richards ("not the tree-climbing Keith Richard"), into deepest Bonymaen. We pass en route the burnt-out shell of the historic Capel-y-Cwm (1820s); destined now for demolition, it replaced a chapel erected here in the 1780s deliberately to thwart the woodland-secluded activities of "the ungodly men of the area [who] would gather on a Sunday to play games, have cockfighting and every sort of merrymaking."

After the war, Spencer's father worked at the post office in Wind Street where he made boxes (he became known as Dai Box), and Mr and Mrs Davies, with their sons Spencer and Paul, moved into a prefab at 3 Cleddau Place, under the northern slope of a then treeless and bare-earth Kilvey Hill. The townspeople called the post-war prefabs "cowsheds", but to Spencer "We had arrived in the lap of luxury, with an airing cupboard you could live in. It had a huge fridge — I'd never seen one before — and my father used to make lollies for us out of government-issue orange juice." The family lived here until about the time Spencer left for London, when they moved to 7 Gors Avenue, Townhill. Cleddau Place no longer exists, the prefabs having been replaced by brick-built houses. "The scene here has changed utterly, and I wouldn't recognise the place if confronted with a photo out of the blue," he says, pinpointing 130 Brokesby Road as roughly the site of his old home.

Before Swansea's early twentieth-century slum clearance resettlements, Bonymaen — or Llanerch, as it was earlier known — was a stronghold of the Welsh language, many of the miners, copper workers, bargemen and small farmers of the area having migrated here from rural west Wales. "But most of the people in the prefabs were from the town, so there wasn't much Welsh," says Spencer. "The more Welsh parts were around Adulam Chapel in Cefn Road and Capel y Cwm."

As we drift into Pentrechwyth and wander past Ogmore Place, he recalls making friends there, aged about 11, with a stamp collector. Still a serious philatelist, he has a collection worth thousands of pounds.

Next stop is the boarded-up, bush-sprouting wreck of Spencer's old Pentrechwyth Junior School. He's amused at a notice that reads "WARNING ANTI VANDAL PAINT USED ON THESE PREMISES" — and at the signs all around us of the warning's ineffectuality: the roof tiles ripped off, the scorch marks, the graffiti, the airgun-pitted aluminium sheets over the school's windows.

At the heart of Bonymaen (Bôn-y-maen: base of the stone), on a grassy bank in front of the Bonymaen Inn, is the four-foot-high *maen*, the ancient standing stone that in coaching days was a landmark on the main road between Swansea and Neath. Nearby, there used to be a *sticil* (stile), a set of steps used by riders to remount their horses after refreshing themselves at the inn in preparation for the steep climb up Cefn Road, in one direction, or Penygraig (Kilvey) in the other. Spencer poses by the *maen*. "Why the fuck you taking pictures of that fuckin' stone?" enquires a lad in a baseball cap. "It's very old," Spencer replies. "So?" "Older than you — older even than us." "It's just a fuckin' stone. Fuck. I'm going for a fuckin' pint."

This seems like a good idea, and we follow him into the Bonymaen Inn, Spencer pointing out the space between the pub's inner and outer doors where, aged 13, he was allowed to busk with his "chest piano". "I was too young to go into the bar, but the drinkers would come out and deposit their coins." This afternoon's clientèle, about a dozen men mostly of Spencer's generation, recognise him instantly — "Spencer Davis! What brings you back to Bonymaen?" — and he recognises many of them: old friends, boys he'd been at school with, a relative or two. He sits down with them and they settle into pondering the Bonymaen of their youth and the land he lives in now. "Big country, America," ventures one. "H'm," muses Spencer, "big country, small minds."

We head finally for Cefn Road, for Spencer to tell me the story of the three-inch scar on the palm of his right hand. Ever on the look-out for means of raising cash, he had a paper round, he grew and sold lettuces, he went spud-bashing in Gower — and then there was the pop bottle scam. At Hopkins' shop in Cefn Road — closed now, but the shuttered serving hatch is still there — you could get money back on your empty bottles. The returned empties were stored in a yard at the rear, and Spencer would tiptoe round the back, help himself to an armful of bottles, carry them round to the hatch at the front — and get "his" money back. All went well until one day his trespassing was rumbled by a yapping dog. He ran for the nearest wall, went to grip the top of it with his right hand — and gashed his palm on the jagged glass that had been set into the wall top. The wound should probably have been stitched, but he dared not tell his parents what had happened, and it was left to heal unaided.

His stamina undiminished, Spencer Davis keeps on running, but, as he sings on *So Far*, "I am not running from my past". With variety and inventiveness on this new album, certain ghosts are laid and positive influences celebrated: "It's been a good ride so far", the Swansea bluesman declares — yet, 67 years down the line, "I got so far to go".

PLANET 180

64

N.J. — A 'Desert Island' Ten

Love — 'Alone Again Or' from *Forever Changes*

A representative track from a favourite album, which I first heard in 1967, soon after its release, I suppose. There seemed to be two West Coast bands in competition for attention at that time, the Doors and Love. Love — the better of the two, in my opinion — somehow failed to get the limelight accorded to the Doors, although the enigmatic Arthur Lee continued to be a cult figure until his death in 2006, soon after he toured with a revived (and notably youthful) Love (they performed a blisteringly magnetic set at the Patti in the summer of 2005). It's a song, and an album, inextricably bound up with memories of being young and idealistic, aged 17/18, in the 'summer of love'. Acoustic guitar, lush orchestral passages and a soaring Spanish (or Mexican) trumpet solo — and simple, even naïve lyrics about 'being in love with almost everyone'. There's a sunniness about the song, but also a sadness and darker shadings, there in the music but also present through association with the 'tormented genius' image which was Arthur Lee's, a labelling which I believe was not mere hype. It conjures up many memories, none of them stronger than listening to the album in a 'secret' drinking club of two or three close friends at school, where we'd light jossticks, play Doors, Love, Stones, Francoise Hardie and Pretty Things albums, get drunk on cooking sherry and talk about love, girls, and our idealistic, hippy-inflected hopes for the future.

Aberjaber — 'Cynghansail Cymru' from *Aberjaber* (LP)

I first heard this instrumental piece being played not by Aberjaber but by Yr Hwntws, as I was walking across the *maes* at the Pontardawe Folk Festival in the late 1970s. I was already a fan of Yr Hwntws, largely because of the rock sensibility they brought to traditional Welsh folk music; they were determinedly breaking from the rather operatic treatments of Welsh folk which tended to be favoured up until that time. I was surprised to hear this seemingly rather 'classical' piece coming from them, and it drew me into the tent to pay closer attention. I thought for a while that it was a version of Pachelbel's 'Canon', to which I had been introduced by Delyth, my (now) former wife, during the early days of our relationship: variations on a lyrical, romantic theme. It turned out not to be Pachelbel's piece but a Welsh traditional theme-and-variation, a curious hybrid of folk music and art music. When Delyth later formed Aberjaber, with Peter Stacey and Stevie Wishart, they recorded a beautiful version of 'Cynghansail Cymru' on their inaugural album.

Jimi Hendrix — 'All Along the Watchtower'

Choosing this one gives me a chance to combine Bob Dylan (a hugely important figure to me) and Jimi Hendrix, who gives us here, I think, the definitive version of Bob Dylan's song. The sheer, orgasmic exuberance of Hendrix's guitar playing is the main reason for choosing this one; the lyrics, in this case, are of secondary significance — indeed, with most of Hendrix's material the instrumental work occupies the foreground, for me, with the lyrics often taking a back seat. This is just as well in some cases: the revolutionary excitement of his guitar playing is sometimes at odds with the traditional macho attitudes of many of the song lyrics. From the distinctive percussive moments of the opening of this song, I am entranced, and remain so throughout: the soaring freedom of the guitar, the wah-wah soloing, the woozy slide zoomings — aural heaven on earth! I suppose most pieces of music, intrinsically compelling as the music is in its own terms, are associated in my mind with particular places, times and people. I think above all, when I hear this number, of the front bar of the

Crown Hotel in Leamington Spa, where my reporter colleagues and I would often pass a liquid lunch hour (or two), and we'd put this Hendrix number on the jukebox again and again. A strong part of the memory of that bar is of a rather beautiful pale girl called Jenny with whom one of my colleagues was quicker to make a go of it than I was; she'll invariably put in a memory appearance when I hear this song.

Miles Davis — 'Time after time' from *You're Under Arrest*, or, alternatively, a passage from *Sketches of Spain*.

There's so much of Miles Davis's considerable oeuvre that I enjoy, from *Kind of Blue* to *Bitches' Brew*, but I am particularly drawn to the open-heart surgery of more melodious pieces such as *Sketches of Spain* and the much later 'Time after time', which he recorded when he was in one of his more rock-inflected moods, towards the end of his life. What exactly was it that Noel Coward said about 'the potency of cheap music'? I have always enjoyed good pop music and I have sometimes relished really *awful* pop music (that Ken and Barbie song, for instance — what a confession, eh? 'Come on, Barbie, let's go party' and all that, which my small daughters and I used to love to sing along to, the sheer daft fun of it). Cindi Lauper, I suppose, falls into the category of really good pop music, and I was utterly smitten by the melody, yearning lyrics and the song's tremendously distinctive, but simple enough bass riff — at the same time as I was intensely involved with a certain American woman. Miles, of course, treats us to a purely instrumental version of the Cindi song, with minimal, perfectly controlled, muted trumpet, strong on melody and strong too on that lovely bass riff. It does indeed conjure up the 'evènements' of a certain summer, but it stands for the hiraeth of anyone's love affair. I *never* play music when I am trying to make a poem, because a poem should be making its own music, and there would be an unseemly clash of two musics were I to put on the radio or a CD while attempting to compose poetry. But I have often used music to get me psyched up *prior* to settling down to work on a poem. When I was trying to write a poem for this particular woman, I would play 'Time after time' after a dozen times before starting work, to get me into precisely the right mood; and if the *awen* wore a bit thin after a couple of hours, I'd play the track again, to reconnect with its spell.

Joni Mitchell — 'A Case of You' from *Blue*

A favourite, representative track from a favourite album. Joni Mitchell's one of the world's great song-writers — a genuine poet and a wonderful melodist, whose songs represent emotional intelligence at its most articulate and poignant: no waffly abstractions and moon/June clichés, but real people in real places with real emotions: 'On the back of a cartoon coaster / In the blue T.V. screen light / I drew a map of Canada …' This album got 'in my blood' like 'holy wine', not long before I went bumming around mainland Europe and North Africa for about a year, and it's associated with many of the places I passed through and the people I met then.

Captain Beefheart — 'Big Eyed Beans from Venus' from *Clear Spot*

Thinking the blues had been done to perfection, Captain Beefheart pushed that music's energies into strange, uncharted, intriguing waters. But the blues are godfather to the best of his work, and his big, grating, compelling blues voice looms large on this wacky track which doesn't pretend to make a lot of conventional sense, but relishes a surreal humour in its weird juxtapositions, and treats us to the ornate syncopations that are so characteristic of the Magic Band's later work. In the middle of the track, Beefheart calls on his guitarist, 'Mr Zoot Horn Rollo, hit that long lingering note and let it float', and Zoot Horn Rollo does precisely that, with a slide-tremulous note that quivers enticingly and at length on its own before the band crashes back in and all glorious musical mayhem breaks loose, until Zoot Horn Rollo rounds off the track with a long, shimmering slide fade-out. The quality of Beefheart's voice is a main pleasure for me. I doubt whether we'd have had Tom Waits without Beefheart blazing a trail for him. I first heard this number at the Oxford Polytechnic (now Oxford Brookes University), when Beefheart and co. were on a European tour in 1974. I was chuffed when my daughter graduated at Oxford Brookes in 2008 to find myself sitting, with other parents, on the self-same stage from which Beefheart had delivered those big-eyed beans thirty odd years earlier. It has enormous, irresistible drive. Whenever I play Beefheart, I have memories of the Edgar Broughton Band, who were friends of mine when I lived in the English Midlands and who probably did more than anyone else to turn me on to Beefheart. Rob (Edgar) Broughton owed a great deal to Beefheart's singing style.

'Myfanwy', by a big Welsh choir

There are numerous clichéd and/or sentimental versions of this classic Welsh love song, but it can be hair-raisingly powerful when delivered by a large male-voice choir. It can also be effective when delivered by a solo baritone voice — John Cale, at grand piano, gives a powerful rendition.

David Ackles — 'Down River' from *Road to Cairo*

I think it may have been John Peel who first alerted me to this very fine American singer-songwriter who released this album in 1968; Ackles followed it up with two other albums, both eagerly awaited by me, and critically though not commercially rewarded, before he died tragically young in the 1970s. I don't know of anyone who has heard of him — apart from Peel (who is now himself dead) and the girl (and her son) I used to live with in Leamington Spa, when I first started playing his records. Ackles is a master of melody and musical arrangements, and writes profoundly affecting lyrics, all the more powerful for their simplicity, restraint and vernacular tone. This is a song told in the first person about someone who meets up with the girlfriend he had before being sentenced to three years in jail. There's a sad, accepting nostalgia to the encounter, the man not blaming her for not writing, and congratulating her on the match she eventually made with an old schoolmate of his. The simple theme of this economically related narrative song, as one of the lines has it, is that 'Times change'. It opens up with a spare honky-tonk piano playing a slow run of minor chords, and gradually, as the emotion builds, the piece wells up into an instrumental conclusion, with drums, swirling organ, and piping lead guitar.

Roy Harper — 'When an old cricketer leaves the crease' from *HQ*
One of the most moving celebrations of (the best sort of) Englishness I have encountered in music, this is a hymn to the culture of village cricket by another neglected song-writing genius, Roy Harper. It's a love song, like many of my choices here, but this time it is basically a love song not just to a game but to a country; it's dedicated, as Harper says in a sleeve note, 'to England my dear home'. I have no interest whatsoever in cricket, but Harper, with his fine skills as a wordsmith, makes the game important to the listener, irrespective of one's interest (or lack of) in sport. There's something hauntingly magical, he persuades us, about village-green cricket:

When an old cricketer leaves the crease
well, you never know whether he's gone
if sometimes you're catching a fleeting glimpse
of a twelfth man at silly mid on
and it could be Geoff or it could be John
with a new ball sting in his tail

and it could be me and it could be thee
and it could be the sting in the tail.

Exquisite writing (if dodgy punctuation). And he has the melody and the arrangement to match it, with a few desultory chords, minimally backing his sweetly melodious voice for about half of the song, and then — sending a shiver down the spine — the entire Grimethorpe Colliery Band comes in, and they're with us for most of the rest of the song. Thus, with the introduction of the colliery band, he effects a fusion of the rural and the urban/industrial, and gives us England whole, rather than the fusty, class-blind, non-urban England of John Major, with its warm beer and old ladies cycling to church.

John Cale — 'Hallelujah' from *Fragments of a Rainy Season*, or, alternatively, 'Riverbank', from *Honi Soit*, or 'Fear'

Two birds with one stone here: Leonard Cohen, one of my favourite song-writers, and John Cale, who, of all the many people who have recorded this song, is the most distinctive. As with his rendition of Presley's 'Heartbreak Hotel', Cale has made it his own. I first heard the song in about 1993, when Cale performed it at the Brangwyn Hall, accompanying himself on grand piano. As with Cale's own lyrics, the song's words work obliquely and create a powerful whole from somewhat disjointed but captivating fragments: love, yearning, time, death, religion — all the big themes are here, and music itself is directly referenced, with a chord change signalled by the lyrics. The melody sweeps you along and registers powerful emotion.

The H'mm Foundation

Nigel Jenkins

'Came for a day/setlo am oes' (stayed a lifetime): this piece of municipal graffiti on the wall of a housing association block in Christina Street, Swansea, speaks poignantly, says Iraqi exile Ali Anwar, to his own condition. Because of political problems with his own government in Baghdad, the then-young student decided in January 1977 to lower the potentially lethal temperature, and took a short break in Swansea, where a close friend from Baghdad was studying. Expecting to spend only a few days in Wales, Ali bought return ticket, but thirty-five years later he still hasn't used the ticket's other half.

It's as well that, having developed a taste for Swansea and Wales, he decided to extend his stay. If he'd returned to Iraq as planned he would almost certainly have been killed. Even so, for several years he was far from safe in his western retreat: the British authorities warned him that he was at risk. But in spite of the long, menacing reach of the Iraqi government, Ali managed to settle in Wales. For years he wanted to find a way of expressing his gratitude to the country that gave him liberty, a home and a family, and now, he believes, that opportunity has come. For over a year, at his own considerable expense, he has been working to establish the H'mm Foundation. Inspired by the bardd teulu or household poet tradition of medieval and Renaissance Wales, the foundation aims to encourage businesses, public bodies, trade unions and other organisations to 'adopt a poet', thereby bridging the gap between poets and the public by showcasing poetry in the workplace, and developing other means of giving poetry a higher profile in people's lives. The foundation was launched in December 2011 at the Wales

Millennium Centre in Cardiff, with speeches from various public figures and politicians, and performances by some of the country's leading poets, among them Gillian Clarke, the National Poet.

'Some people, including poets, see this arrangement as being too good to be true,' Ali told me in an interview in November. 'They suspect that there is some agenda behind the setting up and funding of the H'mm Foundation. They know how busy I am with my own company and life, and they can't believe that I only want to say "Thank you, Wales" for putting up with me and for looking after me these past thirty-five years. It is time, simply, for me to pay back, with interest, and gladly — because I often ask myself, "Who am I without Wales?" I could so easily have been killed, but I wasn't. I have been looked after by the indigenous people and have felt happy to be here.'

I've known Ali since the early 1980s, from a time when Swansea had a livelier political scene than it does today, with vibrant contributions from CND activists, trade unionists, anti-Tories, anti-imperialists, anti-apartheid campaigners, striking steelworkers, refugees from Latin American dictatorships, and exiles from Iraq. There'd be Chile Solidarity nights upstairs in the Coach House in Wind Street; poems-and-pints for flagging devolutionists in the Red Lion, Morriston; 'Free Nelson Mandela' nights in the Cape Horner on Fabian Way. One cause in particular united political activists throughout Wales, namely the miners' strike of 1984-5, during which Ali became friends with many Welsh socialists and nationalists, among them Dafydd Elis Thomas and the MEP David Morris.

Ali Anwar was born in 1957, the sixth of seven children, in a prosperous, close-knit village of some three hundred souls contentedly living among orange trees and date palms about forty miles north of Baghdad. 'If you were to view it from a plane,' says Ali, 'you'd see nothing of the buildings or the people, just the tops of palm trees. The village had a school, a mosque, a small main road with an open market, and a lot of coffee shops.' For generations, from a long way back into Ottoman Empire times, his family on both sides have owned citrus groves in the village of Hwader, on the banks of the River Deiala, which flows from Iran, makes a peninsula of the village and, when it floods every few years, an island. 'Ours was a classic Arab house, just one storey, built around an open courtyard where some orange trees grew, and for four months of the year, during the summer, we'd sleep on the open roof of the house, swathed in the scent of the flowers on the orange trees,' Ali recalls. 'As children, we'd spend hours swimming in the river or playing in the orange groves and climbing date palms — which is a real skill.' His father, who for some years had been head teacher at the village school, was an Arab nationalist with a passion for poetry, which he communicated to Ali at an early age. 'He used to read to us constantly, and encouraged us to recite. Arabic poetry has to rhyme, it's got this musical rhythm to it, which is why I love to hear Welsh and French poetry.'

It was, as he suggests, an idyllic childhood, but ominous clouds began to gather over Ali's riverside Eden. The family had already suffered the death, at age seven, of one of Ali's brothers, when another brother died of leukaemia in Guy's Hospital in London at the age of twenty-four. After that devastating loss, Ali's father had no more stomach for life in Hwader, and the family moved to Baghdad in 1973, when Ali was sixteen. 'I hated Baghdad,' he tells me. 'It was too big. I really missed my friends and the orange groves and the river, and I constantly went back to the village. We kept our house there, but left it locked up after my brother died. It's still there like that.'

The family settled in Baghdad, but during his last year there, he started to think that the situation was too dangerous not only for himself but for his family. 'People started disappearing,' he explains.

'They took our English-language teacher in the school in the village. I thought it was time to take a break, and my father knew it might be better to try to get me out of the country.'

His friend Araf in Swansea had sent him a postcard from Mumbles, extolling the endless Welsh sunshine (it was, after all, the exceptionally dry summer of 1976) and the bikinied delights of Caswell Bay. Araf's reports fused with images from British and American movies to paint a picture in Ali's mind of Swansea as a city of relentless industry, unimaginable nightlife and dreamlike beaches. Although he had never in his life travelled outside Iraq, he decided to pay his friend a surprise visit, completely unannounced.

On arrival at Heathrow, with rudimentary English, Ali found himself in the wrong passport control queue, the one marked 'UK Citizens'. An official gestured to him to join the queue for 'Aliens'. 'I didn't mind at first,' says Ali. 'In fact, the people in the new queue looked more interesting. Then I consulted my pocket dictionary to look up the meaning of "alien". I was rather disappointed. An "alien", it said, was something foreign, not in keeping and quite unlike. I wanted to complain. I wanted to say that I was from Mesopotamia, the first ever civilisation on earth. But I'd only been in Britain for less than ten minutes, so I didn't.'

At Paddington Station, the last train to Swansea had been delayed, luckily for Ali — as otherwise he'd have stayed in London, possibly for good. 'No one told me how long it took to get to Swansea or that Swansea was the last stop on the journey. So I sat next to the window and read the name of the station every time the train stopped. I very nearly got out at Swindon.' The only other passenger in Ali's carriage was, it turned out, a Swansea woman who chatted cheerily away the whole journey. Not that Ali understood much, but he did learn from her that Swansea was at the end of the line. 'I was expecting to arrive at somewhere like New York,' he says, 'all Marilyn Monroe, casinos, steam blooming up from the pavements. But when I arrived at

Swansea, at two o'clock on a January morning, it was totally, totally dead. There were only two taxis on the rank and both drivers were fast asleep.'

As Ali's friend had mentioned Swansea's seafront hotels, he asked one of the taxi drivers to find him one. They scoured the seafront as far as Mumbles and back, but every B&B they stopped at was either full or closed for the night. "No room at the inn," the taxi driver kept saying in between telling jokes and trying to make conversation with me. I kept consulting my dictionary, trying in vain to answer him. I asked him to write the jokes down on a piece of paper so that my Iraqi friend could translate them for me. He was laughing his head off, his big belly nudging the steering wheel. One of his jokes was: "If your nose goes on strike, what do you do to it? You pick it." I told him strikes were not allowed in Iraq. At this stage he was laughing so much that he had to stop the car and get out to finish his laughter.'

They pulled up outside Swansea University. 'I still haven't seen the sea,' Ali remarked. 'There's the fucking sea,' said the taxi driver, stabbing a finger seawards. So, as the driver waited for him, Ali wandered off towards the sound of the sea. 'It smelt foul, polluted, and I had a horrible splashing from it, and worried that the driver wouldn't let me back into the taxi. But he did.'

The only inn with room for Ali was the poshest in town, the Dragon Hotel. Dropping Ali off there, the taxi driver refused to accept the by-now hefty fare. 'I have had a lovely time,' he told Ali, 'I couldn't possibly accept your money.' When Ali later informed his family in Baghdad that he'd been staying in the Dragon Hotel in a country which had a dragon on its flag, they thought these were worryingly bad omens, as the dragon in Arab culture has distinctly negative associations.

Swansea may not have been New York, but the city continued to surprise Ali. When he went to NatWest Bank to deposit the cash he'd brought with him from Iraq, who should serve him but the woman who'd been his companion on the train from Paddington. And a girl he later dated turned out to be the daughter of that selfsame woman. 'If you made this up for a piece of fiction, you'd be laughed at,' he says.

After a few days, having met up with Araf, he decided to stay in Swansea and, with his father's financial support, enrolled on a course at Swansea Institute (now Swansea Metropolitan University). He had to register at the central police station and report once a month to the 'Aliens Department', where he and his Iraqi friend discovered that they appeared to have Welsh names. 'Your name, Anwar,' the officer informed Ali, 'means uncultivated and uncivilised, and your friend's name, Araf, means slow.' (They were the first Welsh words that Ali learned.) 'It's no big thing to be called an alien,' continued the officer. 'Our Prince Philip was an alien.'

Ali lived for a while in Glanmor Road, Uplands, where his nationalist landlord operated a clandestine radio service in Welsh. 'At night time,' Ali recalls, 'he'd go up the ladder with his aerial and I would hold the ladder in the freezing cold, while his friend inside made the broadcast. I learned a lot from him about the language and the culture, and it was through him that I first heard of the Mabinogion.'

Ali's fascination with the Mabinogion would eventually see him translating into Arabic all eleven prose tales, a four-year project, with a collaborator in London, which was completed in 2009. 'The Mabinogion is unknown in the Arab world, just as Wales is unknown. It's talking about a time when there was no connection with the Arabs and the Muslims whatsoever. One of my problems with the translation was the spelling of the many Welsh names, so I devised a table to be used as a guide for the pronunciation of Welsh names in Arabic.' Finding a publisher has not been easy. There were promising negotiations with one in Beirut, but they eventually came to nothing. Many Arabic publishing houses are specialising increasingly in religious texts, and have little interest in secular volumes.

However, Ali thinks he has found a publisher for a reduced, pilot volume, consisting of the four core tales known as Pedair Cainc y Mabinogi.

Ali enjoyed living in the Uplands, drinking at the Uplands Tavern, buying fish and chips at Mr D's, and relishing the company of a widening circle of Welsh friends. 'I found myself in a small village environment and felt very much at home,' he recalls. Implacably opposed to the Iran-Iraq war between 1980 and 1988, Ali found himself called upon frequently to address political gatherings and the students' union about the political situation in the Middle East. 'I now see that I went too public about it, and this had consequences, not least for my family back home in Iraq.'

He moved house regularly, often staying with Chilean friends who had been granted political asylum in Swansea following Pinochet's 1973 coup. Eventually he moved to the village of Murton, on the edge of Bishopston, some six miles into Gower. There, in a cul-de-sac of bungalows called Miles Lane, he found himself in congenial political company with Harry Stratton, a veteran of the Spanish Civil War. He met Harry through the taxi driver who had driven him around Swansea the night he'd arrived in 1977. When Ali had pitched up at the railway station not long afterwards, the taxi driver had greeted him like a long-lost friend, and introduced him to his best mate Harry, who also drove a cab. This was Harry Stratton, the author of a 1985 civil war memoir entitled *To Anti-Fascism by Taxi*.

In the meantime, Ali had started working at Swansea Institute — as a teacher initially, and then as an information technology consultant at the Swansea University Innovation Centre. He was also seeing Karen, who came from a Staffordshire mining family; they would eventually set up home together and have two daughters, Lauren Nadia and Kathryn Layla. Ali was granted British citizenship in 1987. When an IT project at the Innovation Centre was concluded in 1989, he was given permission to adopt the venture as a limited company, initially with just two employees. Later Karen became his partner in the company. Today, his company, CADCentre (UK) Ltd, with its head office in Swansea, employs 112 people in ten branches across Wales and southern England, providing skills-building IT programmes and apprenticeships in the business administration, engineering and manufacturing sectors. The company is one of the few training organisations in Wales that delivers all its courses in Welsh as well as English, and at the annual Wales Business Awards, organised by the Institute of Welsh Affairs and the *Western Mail*, it sponsors a national award for the use of Welsh in the workplace.

As a successful businessman with a commodious residence in Cardiff, thoughts still come to mind about those notorious questions of identity on the British census form. Is he an 'Alien', a 'Foreigner', 'Another' or 'Another (please specify)'? 'You think,' says Ali, 'what are you? An authentic other, an elsewherer? When I die, where am I to be buried? My Iraqi family would expect me to be buried in Iraq. But I have a family here too. Who, indeed, am I without Wales?'

It is through literature, and poetry in particular, that he has chosen to pay the debt he feels he owes to Wales. The H'mm Foundation echoes the title of R.S. Thomas's 1972 collection *H'm* — Thomas being one of Ali's favourite poets. Prior to the official launch of the foundation, the initiative had a string of informal presentations, with poetry readings at various conferences and cultural events. There were about a dozen such events, including Gillian Clarke at the IWA's 'Inspire Wales' awards in Cardiff; Robert Minhinnick at a conference of broadcasters; Dave Hughes at the 'Children First' conference in Cardiff; Mike Jenkins at a conference about the south Wales valleys; Menna Elfyn at the Wales Business Awards, and Karen Owen at the Institute of Directors' Christmas lunch in

Llandudno. In every case, the poetry was well received.

The launch of the H'mm Foundation on 7 December featured a crowded Glanfa auditorium at the Millennium Centre, with an eclectic roster of poets, musicians and other public figures, among them Gillian Clarke, Menna Elfyn, David Hughes, Ifor Thomas, Jon Gower, Margot Morgan, Andy Jones, Angharad Jenkins, Huw Williams, Bethan Rhiannon Williams-Jones, Peter Stead, Dr Barry Morgan, Alan Edmunds of Media Wales, Robert Lloyd Griffiths of the Institute of Directors Wales, Geraint Talfan Davies of the IWA and Lleucu Siencyn of Literature Wales.

Ali hopes that from the launch onwards the financing of this ambitious project will devolve to companies and organisations that have committed themselves to 'adopt a poet'. The first to do so was the *Western Mail*, which adopted its weekly columnist Menna Elfyn as its bardd teulu. A poet's engagement with a company might be as brief as a lunchtime reading to staff, or there could be more extensive commitments, such as writing workshops and residencies. With about forty poets on his list so far, and growing interest from the business community, Ali hopes that the H'mm Foundation will become self-financing in 2012, with sufficient funds to relieve him of the administrative chores.

Welsh poetry in both languages has been Ali's greatest inspiration. 'In an R.S. Thomas poem about Raymond Garlick called "Commission", he explains, 'there's a piece about Raymond Garlick being Welsh by choice and not by birth. The poet writes: "Welsh not by birth, but for a better reason/ Birth being compulsory and not chosen,/ As you chose this: to live here and be kind/ To our speech, learning it, and to our race,/ Who have God's pardon but have not His peace...'

'This is how I feel,' says Ali. 'It's really my good fortune that has brought me to these shores. For the past ten years I could have lived anywhere, so it's by choice that I am here. The only thing I regret is that my Welsh is not good enough and my Arabic is terrible because I don't use it enough. But I am a very happy resident at Hotel Gwales, listening to the birds of Rhiannon, enjoying the company of Branwen and Manawydan, while the unwise hand of Heilyn son of Gwyn hasn't yet opened door number three, that Cornwall-facing door. I'm settling down well at the Hotel Gwales, where there has indeed been a welcome at the inn, and there is so much for me to write home about.'

His mother's last words to him before Ali left Iraq had been, 'Mind your own business and be careful with strangers.' It's as well for Wales that he didn't take her advice too literally, for Ali Anwar's contribution as an informed and active participant in the life of the country has been exemplary.

PLANET 205

Damned for Dreaming

Nigel Jenkins profiles the Algerian writer and journalist Soleïman Adel Guémar who has settled in Swansea.

At the end of the Swansea-centred UK Year of Literature and Writing 1995, there were hopes that Swansea might join the network of international Cities of Refuge for persecuted writers, becoming thereby Britain's first such city. The plan advanced by the festival's projectors was that the local authority would combine with various arts bodies to provide a persecuted writer with a safe haven in Swansea and the wherewithal to pursue his or her literary career. Like many a Swansea plan, it came to nothing. But in 2003, unofficially and fortuitously, Swansea did indeed become a writer's city of refuge when Soleïman Adel Guémar, whose courageous investigative journalism had provoked threats to his life in his native Algiers, settled there with his family. By 2007, when his substantial bilingual collection *State of Emergency/État d'Urgence* appeared, it was being acknowledged, to quote Lisa Appignanesi of English PEN in her introduction to the book, that "Britain has inadvertently inherited a political poet of stature, one whose language sings."

Published in Algeria and France, as both a poet and short-story writer, and the winner of two national poetry prizes, Adel Guémar was little known in Britain — outside Swansea literary circles — until the publication of *State of Emergency* in Arc Publications' much admired "Visible Poets" series, which aims to make "visible" to an English-reading public poets who have significant reputations in their homeland, but whose work has been infrequently translated beyond their borders. Winner of an English PEN Writers in Translation Award, the collection is translated by Tom Cheesman and John Goodby, of Swansea University's German and English departments respectively; they have striven to recreate in their resourceful yet faithful versions the artful lucidity, the sensuous atmosphere, the sometimes surreal strangeness that distinguish the French originals — while resisting the (common) temptation to confect poems that read as though they had originally been written in English. The book, well received by reviewers, has led to Adel Guémar being invited to read at venues and festivals all over Britain, his poetry delivering "the news that stays news" about a country whose protracted, murderous turmoil is only fitfully reported in the British media.

Although 130 years of French colonialism were brought to an end by the War of Independence (1954-62), Algeria's troubles were by no means over: to date, some 200,000 people have been killed in the internecine strife that has continued to mark Algeria as a profoundly dysfunctional country. "The dreams of the revolution were betrayed, and they continue to be betrayed up to the present," says Adel, who was born in Algiers in 1963 to parents who, as militant anti-colonialists and left-wingers, had met in the *maquis* during the war. With his mother a teacher and his father on the staff of the national oil company, Sonatrach, his was a well-connected middle-class family, many scholars and military top-brass — including, during the 1990s, the head of the navy — being numbered among his relatives, not that such a background was any earnest of security. The Minister of Defence during the War of Independence, who was married to Adel's aunt, fell out of favour after independence when he joined the opposition, and was assassinated by the regime on a visit to Germany. In 1969, Adel's immediate family, who lived in a commodious villa in El-Biar, Algiers, were driven out of their house by the police, who then gave it to Cherif Messaadia, the hard-line boss of the Front de Libération Nationale. "All the family suffered a lot," says Adel, "but we were among many, many others who suffered similar if not worse things. Nobody in Algeria is untouched by the violence." Thereafter, his parents — both of the Kabyle line of Berbers — kept their heads down and concentrated on providing for the family.

In spite of such shadows, his was a notably happy childhood. "All my happiness — this sun inside myself — comes from this family," says Adel. "Even when I spent three months in military prison in 1987, and it was very, very hard, I was nevertheless very happy, because of the happiness, strength and confidence my family gave me. Love has been the main parameter of my life. Love and war, love and justice — these are the main subjects of my poetry. Love is a dream and justice is a dream."

The stubborn persistence of that love and the tenacity with which he cleaves to the ideals of the revolution form the foundation on which he constructs his poetry's socio-political forensic. No matter how bleak or horrific the matter beneath his unflinching gaze, he refuses to settle for the comforts of despair — which have exculpated many a poet, in both life and art, from any further exertions — and insists on the potency of that favoured word "dream", not as an unrealisable, solipsist fantasy but as aspiration, the emboldening, subversive goal of a "dream-Algiers". The inspirational "dream" may embody a wholesome memory from the past, or some simple, human pleasure snatched from the edgy present ("to drink/a cup of black coffee near the port/and gaze out facing the sea"), or a vision of some day in the future when "the bayonets will serve/for nothing". Against the reductive, brutal agencies of corrupt power and fanatical fundamentalism he advances energies such as the ensorcelling "beauty/of the starry sky and the candour/of newborns", rather as Lorca in 1930s Spain countered the routine thuggery of the Civil Guard with the sensuality and abundant lyricism of the Gypsies. He feels the desire to

act as if everything was possible

for the child who used to wish
Algiers to be the loveliest of all the brides

— and he laments as he rages against too many a "childhood snatched away/in the streets of Algiers". Given the significance to the poet of family, it is not surprising that Adel has chosen to dedicate his book to his parents, his wife and children, and "all those whose dreams have survived the scourge of human stupidity". The last poem in his book asks of Algeria, "will you ever bear/the child I expect of you".

As with many a sensitive teenager, it was love that first stung Adel into song, aged thirteen, using classical metric forms, to which he continued to resort in the café *chansons* he performed with his guitar in the 1980s. One of these lyrics — "Anniversaire", written in rhyming alexandrines — is included in *State of Emergency*, where otherwise a short-lined, unpunctuated free verse prevails. He wrote initially in both French and Arabic, but he has written no poetry in Arabic — apart from a recent poem about Gaza — for twenty-five years. "I have felt freer writing poetry in French," he says. "Arabic has been used by the regime to tell so many lies." He continues to write love poems, often of an exuberant lyricism, and instinct with a longing for the unremarkable joys of normality; but his innate romanticism is frustrated, as is "ordinary" life, by grim political realities. His position is akin to Pablo Neruda's, in his famous poem of the Spanish Civil War, "I explain a few things": when asked where in his poetry were the lilacs and the poppy-petalled metaphysics, Neruda could only crescendo "Come and see the blood in the streets." Similarly, Adel, on his path "through gardens trampled/by the fury of men", declares himself

[...] guilty of being horrified
by all the massacres crimes

85

against humanity committed
unpunished at my door

Having studied maths, engineering and electronics, he embarked on what turned out to be a short-lived military career. "For political reasons," he says, "I was not proud to wear the uniform. In the military, the generals and the colonels considered themselves the masters of the people." Having made plain his desire to quit the army and having been incarcerated in a military prison, he was nevertheless invited to become a member of the Sécurité Militaire. "I refused. It was a criminal organisation. It is against the people, democracy and freedom."

In 1989, he left Algiers and spent two years working for a publishing company in Paris. The situation at home seemed to improve in 1991, when the Government "gave democracy" to no fewer than 63 parties; so Adel returned in 1992, beginning a new career as a journalist. But the apparent democratisation was a sham, marking the beginning of what Adel calls "the war against civilians", which has been waged not only against the defenders of human rights but against the people in general. Algeria's *capitalisme sauvage* — which might be translated as "feral capitalism" — has virtually wiped out the middle class, creating a bipolar nation of billionaires (many of them former Islamist activists) and paupers.

He worked initially for a government newspaper and then for *L'Évenément*, before becoming an independent journalist, filing stories for a range of publications and setting up a publishing company with the intention of producing his own newspaper — a plan forestalled by government restrictions. His fearless investigation of corruption and atrocities exposed him to the "attentions" of government and Islamist fundamentalists alike, and by the late 1990s friends were growing anxious about the safety of both Adel and his family — he and his wife Latéfa, an electronics engineer whom he had married in 1993, having by this time given birth to two children, Imène (b. 1995) and Nadji (b. 1997). Along with human rights watchdogs, investigative journalists are feared by the regime as its most formidable adversaries: about seventy journalists have been murdered. Shortly before the Guémars fled, Adel reported on a colleague who met a horrific death after exposing corruption in a town bordering Tunisia. The journalist was attached to the rear of a car belonging to the chairman of the local chamber of commerce, dragged around the streets, tortured for three days, made to drink acid, and dumped; he then committed suicide. Adel knew it was time to leave when the door to his flat was kicked in, the place was ransacked, files were destroyed, and he was attacked by knife-wielding goons believed to be associated with the regime: "If I had stayed in Algeria, I would have been dead by now, and perhaps my family would be too."

Although neither Adel nor members of his immediate family have suffered personally the worst that the regime can throw at dissidents, his poetry is proof that his contact with those who have endured imprisonment, torture, maiming, and the murder or "disappearance" of loved ones has equipped his imagination to inhabit warped humanity's darkest corners — from Algeria to Gaza to Guantánamo Bay. As his translators observe in their preface, "For Guémar, Algeria is not just a microcosm but an important laboratory of the worldwide 'War on Terror.'" In several dramatic monologues he deploys an invented first-person voice to give harrowing expression to victims of state violence, as in "Vengeance":

particular soldiers
disfigured the face of my beloved
dead for having believed freedom
possible

the Berlin Wall fell far from us
even as we were singing
of an earlier victory [i.e. national independence]
so very quickly confiscated

I've no desire to beg pardon
of my torturers — as if! —
I've no desire to close my eyes

The reader is spared nothing, in an excruciatingly direct poem such as "Gégène", and the torturers are damned conclusively by their actions:

these lost eyes
this shaven skull
these broken teeth
this nose that bleeds

this naked body
is sitting
on the neck of a bottle

Yet the poet understands that such monstrous deeds also damage the torturer: "the rising of this inhuman stench/contaminates my torturers/and the whole world". Scarcely less culpable are the self-absorbed careerists, the turners of blind eyes, and those who distract themselves with the comforts of consumerism, in circles where "a man is worth less than a glass of whisky":

of course words exist
to hide the horror
familiar gentle music

does the rest

If the poet's words, on the other hand, confront the horror with unshrinking resolve, the experience of these poems is not one of unrelieved bleakness. The honesty of his gaze and his defiant anger are in themselves restorative. Then there's his deep, subversive vein of comedy, from wry asides such as:

only yesterday
the butcher gave me a dirty look
as he served me half a pound
of cat
wrapped in newspaper
— it was the front page
and the president looked very proud

— to the gallows humour of "I listen to old mosquitoes dancing/ around stains of spilt blood". He has a satirist's eye for grotesque mismatches between word and deed, pretension and reality, as when he notes the Minister for Trade's double chin as the politician informs television viewers that "a fridge is a luxury", or the relief with which some general scratches his crotch as his underlings fawningly salute, one of many apt metaphors for the arrogance of power. He relishes absurdism ("huge-eyed/conquerors /on chocolate thrones") and topsy-turvydom ("a brass band playing true fake tunes/the better to deceive"), and takes a Swiftian delight in burlesque but deadpan overstatement — a notable feature of his remarkable short-story collection, *Local Therapy*, which has yet to find an English-language publisher.

It was in December 2002 that Adel, having left Latéfa and the children in Algiers for the time being, applied for asylum at Heathrow. He stayed in London initially with his two brothers, who had already sought asylum there (he has a sister similarly exiled in Paris), and then, when Latéfa and the children were able to join him, in a hostel for some months. Shortly after the birth of their third child, Lina, in 2003, the Home Office "dispersed" the Guémars to Swansea — a city of which they had barely heard. They were allocated a council house in Penlan, one of Wales's most impoverished communities, where they waited anxiously, until 2005, for the government to grant them asylum and indefinite leave to stay. Their tension was augmented by various racist incidents, in what is an area notorious for its coolness towards those who are perceived to be "outsiders". Youths threw eggs at their house, Adel's tyres were repeatedly slashed and the children were sometimes subjected to unpleasant comments at school. "They didn't accept strangers, even if you were from another part of Britain or from somewhere else in Wales," says Adel. The situation grew so stressful that the family asked to be relocated. In 2007, they moved to a council house in Upper Killay, within a few hundred yards of Fairwood Common and one of the "gateways" to Gower, where they have settled happily. In spite of the mixed experience of Penlan, Swansea has generally given the Guémars a warm welcome, says Adel: "Swansea is part of Algiers, that's how I see it — the sea, the people. I didn't feel myself a stranger here in spite of having very little English at first."

The politics of his beloved homeland, as well as political developments elsewhere in the world, continue to absorb the poet, but the experience of recent years has given him a new, related subject: the hiraeth of exile. "Although my brothers and sister left Algeria a long time ago, I never thought that I would have to leave Algeria and live as an exile," says Adel, whose "office" is the kitchen table, where he chain-smokes as he writes, plays his guitar, or watches Al Jazeera on his laptop, to keep abreast of news from the Arab world. To return in safety to a free, just, democratic Algeria is his fondest dream; but the "emergency" has been unconscionably enduring, and there is little hope of its ending soon. Latéfa, who works in Swansea University's adult education department, spent a month there last year, and found the situation steadily worsening. While others "have to stay/for the necessary hope/for the necessary mourning", Adel finds himself obliged to bide his time:

> *where the sun*
> *shines less gently [...]*
> *but the very greyness tunes*
> *the strings of sad guitars*
> *born under the wandering star*
> *damned to the end of time*
> *for having committed dreams*
> *deep in overcrowded dead-ends*

Like Lorca and Neruda, or Brecht in Germany, Hikmet in Turkey, Miłosz in Poland, Soleïman Adel Guémar has been important enough to his country for its misrulers to have wanted him, dead or alive, out of the way. One hopes that the poet-in-exile is able to draw some consolation from the likelihood that in the sane and stable homeland he yearns for he will be seen to have performed for Algeria a uniquely creative act of "national service".

MOMENT DE VÉRITÉ
sous l'arbre allongé
je contemple le ciel gris
qui se fissure en de petits tapis persans

les feuilles au-dessus de moi
frémissent et tombent
frénétiquement
me couvrent

je revois passer ma vie
comme si la mort
m'attendait de pied ferme
au sortir de mes rêveries

j'ai arrêté de m'inventer
des personnages
qui n'arrivaient même pas
à m'amuser

seul
je me regarde
dans le ciel gris

MOMENT OF TRUTH
Lying under a tree
I contemplate a grey sky
Split into little Persian carpets

The leaves overhead
Shake and fall
Frantically
And cover me

I see my life passing before me
As if death
Is surely waiting for me
As my daydreams end

I have stopped inventing
Characters
Who just don't entertain me
Anymore

Alone
I look at myself
In the grey sky

MARÉE BASSE
dunes divinement pointées au ciel
caressées par une brise languissante
souffle chaud saccadé
a mesure que lentement s'élève
et s'affaisse — va et vient mélodieux —
un homme revenu de loin

parcourant l'étendue veloutée
une éternité durant
il boit d'une source immaculée

parfumée a l'encens
qui lui fait tourner la tête
douce la voix exige
de lui qu'il s'étende
et se laisse faire
tandis que les étoiles
deviennent indiscrètes

-2-

sur la plage de Swansea
nos corps enlacés
redécouvrent la danse des cignes
et nous entrons en transe
toi la première
paupières frémissantes
le front ruisselant
sur mes lèvres

et je me remets a tousser
souvenir des nuits agitées
quand je fumais pour éteindre
le feu qui brûlait en moi

— se détache de l'obscurité
entre ciel et terre
dans toute sa splendeur
une ville martyre que je ne reverrai peut-être plus
où la beauté se mêle a la fureur
la musique à la peur des bombes —

d'instinct tu le devines

ta main efface mes visions
tes yeux limpides
me ramènent a ton île

LOW TIDE
dunes divinely pointed to the sky
caressed by a languid breeze
hot breath in fitful time
with the slow rise
and fall — melodious back and forth —
of a man returned from afar

across the velvety expanse
for an eternity
he drinks from an immaculate spring
scented with incense
which makes him turn his head

the gentle voice insists
that he stretch himself out
and let it be done
while the stars
become indiscreet

-2-

on Swansea beach
our hugging bodies
rediscover the swans' dance
and we go into a trance
you first

eyelashes trembling
forehead streaming
on my lips

and I start coughing again
remembering the agitated nights
when I smoked to put out
the fire burning in me

— emerging from the darkness
between sky and land
in all its splendour
a martyr city I may never see again
where beauty mingles with fury
music with the fear of bombs —

by instinct you guess
your hand effaces my visions
your limpid eyes
take me to your island

PLANET 194

Only when it's gone

Nigel Jenkins is worried about the future of Swansea's Dylan Thomas Centre

Swansea is notorious, in the words of Joni Mitchell, for "not knowing what it's got 'til it's gone". Now there are fears that the Dylan Thomas Centre, in the heart of the city's maritime quarter, is poised to suffer the fate of the much lamented Mumbles railway.

There have always been rumours about the Centre's prospects, but since late 2010 the whispers and murmurs have swirled disturbingly, fuelled by an apparent reluctance on the Council's part, in spite of several opaque if not contradictory press releases, to come clean about their intentions for the building, its programme and its 22 members of staff.

I understand the latest version of 'the plan' is for the building to be taken over by the troubled University of Wales on 1 May. However, the extent to which it might remain purposefully a Dylan Thomas Centre — with the exhibition and literary programme intact — remains uncertain. Those involved in the changes that are undoubtedly underway in how the Centre should be run in the future should state their intentions clearly.

For the best part of 17 years, since it was opened by former United States President Jimmy Carter during the UK 1995 Year of Literature and Writing, the Centre has been at the heart of the burgeoning Dylan Thomas 'industry', said to be worth some £3.5 million a year to Swansea's economy.

The Centre has a permanent exhibition about the life and work of Dylan Thomas, a bookshop, and is a venue for lectures and other events. Indeed, it has delivered a rolling programme of literary and artistic events unparalleled for its variety and excellence by any other arts venue in the United Kingdom. The Centre has celebrated the literatures of Wales, in addition to music, drama and the visual arts. It has attracted to Swansea a panoply of internationally renowned writers who, returning home, have burnished the renown of Swansea and Wales in all parts of the world.

Plans are currently being laid, locally and nationally, for celebrations of the one hundredth anniversary, in 2014, of the birth of Dylan Thomas, Swansea's most famous son. The city is surely going to look a little bizarre, to put it mildly, in the eyes of the wider world if it is seen to have abandoned the Dylan Thomas Centre on the eve of this major national and international celebration.

If the Council is determined to unburden itself of the Dylan Thomas Centre, one possible way of doing so — if the current rumoured plan comes to naught — would be to invite interested parties to form a trust to run the Centre, in the same way as a trust was formed to run Swansea's refurbished Leisure Centre. Among them would be many of the well over 200 writers, artists and long-time supporters of the Centre who have launched a petition in its support.

In the past the Dylan Thomas Centre has been run as a compartmentalised rather than as a unified concern. This means it has enormous, untapped potential. It needs the kind of coherent, imaginative vision that would be likely to flow from a group of dedicated and informed trustees, as is the case with all sorts of arts venues, from the Munster Literature Centre in Swansea's twin city of Cork to the wonderfully vibrant Chapter Arts Centre in Cardiff.

IWA – The Welsh Agenda online 30th March 2011

The Man Who Saw Everything Twice

Nigel Jenkins on the art of Evan Walters

The return to Swansea this August of the National Eisteddfod, which in 1926 awarded a joint first prize for art to Evan Walters (1893-1951), has prompted the city's Glynn Vivian Art Gallery to mount a retrospective exhibition of work by the locally-born painter: Evan Walters: *Moments of Vision*, 20 June-20 August. It will give the viewing public an opportunity to assess the justice, or otherwise, of David Bell's 1952 summation of Walters as "a great artist who never painted a great picture".

Evan Walters had had to resign from the 1926 Eisteddfod's Arts and Crafts Committee in order to enter the competition which was judged by Augustus John (1878-1961) who, although a fervent advocate of the younger man's earlier work, regretted its limited use of colour. The prize-winning painting, in the category "Castle without people", was a study of Pennard Castle under lowering Gower skies — which is indeed tonally subdued, like much of Walters' earlier work. Solidly representational, it can be seen as fitting in to a well-established tradition of Gower water colours and oils, and there is little doubt that Walters, an unusually accomplished draughtsman, could have made a cosy reputation for himself — and a comfortable living — as a producer of pleasing landscapes and reliable portraits. But, ever disinclined to fulfil conventional expectations, and restlessly experimental, he went on to plough a highly individualistic and often lonely furrow, producing a formidable body of work in remarkably varied, if not antithetical, styles.

Presented with half a dozen paintings selected more or less at random from Walters' *oeuvre*, a viewer unfamiliar with his work would surely be tempted to attribute each one to a different artist, such was Walters' impatience with artistic pigeonholing and his appetite for innovation. Walters is like a Welsh equivalent of the "multifarious" Portuguese poet Fernando Pessoa (1888-1935), who wrote such incongruent styles of poetry that he invented names and distinct identities for the different kinds of poet that, at certain times, he chose to be. This sheer variety — in a critical climate which tended then, as now, to favour the cultivation and anxious retention of a single, readily identifiable "voice" — often counted against Walters, alienating both traditionalists and those with more avant-garde pretensions. Reviewing the Glynn Vivian's posthumous exhibition in 1952, Goronwy Powell wrote in *The Western Mail* that Walters "ignored all contemporary artistic trends and past traditions to pursue his own arbitrary and utterly individualist line, regardless of the cost to his reputation... [His] successive revolutionary changes of form and style over nearly 40 years can be seen only too clearly in the current memorial exhibition." Powell complained of "bewildering, sad distortions of masterly work" which were "sufficient to show his dangerous versatility". Some of the work of which Powell was most dismissive, such as *Stout Man with a Jug* (1936) and *Self-Portrait with Candle* (c. 1939), may now be seen, in the light of recent, more eclectic critical approaches, as among the most impressive of the paintings that emerged from Walters' famous and somewhat obsessive "binocular" experiments. It is no longer an adequate critical response to select the Walters that flatters one's tastes and to disdain the rest of his output as an aberration. Over fifty years after his death, he deserves to be seen whole, in all his multifarious vitality, as one of the most significant — and under-appreciated — artists of twentieth-century Wales.

Few Welsh painters have been more unequivocally and self-consciously The Artist. The *Self Portrait with Candle*, as a wordless yet combatively articulate manifesto, sets out his stall. There he takes his stand, the Artist, capital "A", at binocular war with what he called "that dull robot the camera": the black halo of his beret, the Daliesque moustache and the imperial tuft of beard declaring for Art, and the refulgence generated in paint by those multiplying candles outshining that of the mere sun, glancing palely off what seems to be his right cheek (but which, of course, is his mirror-reflected left). Out of the frame, what seems to be his left hand, but which is his right, works its restless, incendiary magic, while those haughty, defiant eyes insist that no matter how much the critics, the public and his patrons scorn his experiments, the revolution will not be thwarted. As the younger Swansea painter Alfred Janes (1911-99) remarked at the time of Walters' death: "Everything that the public expects from an artist Evan gave them in a big way. He was colourful, boisterous, hail fellow well met and most important — he occasionally administered to convention the salutary shock of which it's in such dire need."

Evan John Walters was born — the youngest of three surviving children (a fourth, born after him, died in early childhood) — at the Welcome Inn, Mynyddbach, in the parish of Llangyfelach. The area today, to the traveller turning off the M4 in the direction of Swansea, seems little more than a suburban blur, architecturally characterless apart from the ghost of a village centre represented by the Plough and Harrow pub and, nearby, the rebuilt church of St Cyfelach (1830s) with its detached Norman tower. A century ago, it was a distinctive, thriving, entirely Welsh-speaking community; although separated by only a few miles from the industrial and commercial ferment of Swansea, it was predominantly rural, with the odd colliery, such as Cefngyfelach, standing out among the farms. Evan's mother managed the Welcome Inn, while his father worked as a carpenter. He seems to have enjoyed a happy childhood, with every encouragement from his parents, particularly from his mother, to pursue artistic ambitions — unusual, not to say unrealistic, in a working-class context at that time — which were evident from almost the outset. At the age of two, he was drawing with chalk on the kitchen floor, and by the time he was ten he was touting his skills around social events in the locality, selling portraits sketched on postcards for a few pence each. While serving as an apprentice painter and decorator, having left school at the age of thirteen, he found himself in demand as a painter of inn signs and, for a shilling apiece, of colliers' greyhounds.

Funds raised from the sale of signed paintings helped him enrol, in 1906, as an evening student at the Swansea School of Art. The subsequent award of a scholarship enabled him, by the age of sixteen, to become a full-time student at the school, whose visionary new principal, the Scotsman W. Grant Murray (1877-1950), was determined to forge a trend-setting reputation for the fledgling institution, and to use the scholarship system to create new opportunities for working-class students. Arriving for interview with a sample of his work in hand, Walters made an immediate impact. "[He] was dressed in shabby clothes with a colourful handkerchief round his neck and on his head a cap which he did not remove, pulled down to one side," recorded one of the lecturers who, with Grant Murray, conducted the interview. "The first impression was that he was a gypsy lad. His speech seemed to be a mixture of Welsh and English and we had great difficulty in understanding him. His picture was, he stated, done with ordinary house paints." From the time that Grant Murray helped him obtain a place at the Regent Street Polytechnic — whence, in 1914, he was admitted to the Royal Academy Schools — London would play an increasingly important role in his career, although Llangyfelach and Swansea would continue to exert a magnetic pull, sometimes for long periods. But his relationship with London had to wait to mature: in 1915, he left for the United States, serving as a camouflage painter with the American army when the United States entered the war, and not returning to Britain until 1918.

He seems to have produced little work in the United States, but by 1920 he had amassed sufficient paintings and drawings to mount his first one-man show — at the Glynn Vivian, which, under Grant Murray's direction, was attracting unprecedented attention to the arts in Swansea. The exhibition, featuring landscapes, portraits, genre subjects and works with religious themes — categories that would remain central to his art — won instant popular and critical acclaim, with the local press lionising this "prophet at home" in a manner that would continue for the rest of his life. Among those captivated by this prodigious new talent was "Mam o Nedd", the eisteddfodic name of the prominent social reformer, Liberal and champion of the arts Winifred Coombe Tennant (1874-1956) of Cadoxton, Neath. She took Walters under her wing and was instrumental in securing him commissions to paint the portraits of such figures as Lloyd George, Ramsey Macdonald and Lord Balfour. "Here was genius," she later wrote, "I saw that at once — genius still in the stage where it is striving to express itself and conscious of the difficulty of mastering a technique." A decisive factor in the development of Walters' career, her patronage continued until the end, in spite of her exasperation with his later binocular experiments.

The high-point of the 1921-31 period, during which Walters exhibited annually in the Royal Academy's summer exhibitions, was a one-man show at the Warren Gallery, London in 1927. Partly, no doubt, because of Augustus John's imprimatur and some patronising promotional nonsense about the artist's untutored backwoods origins, the crowds flocked to admire the works of this "primitive" Celt, and Walters became an overnight celebrity. He could hardly have wished for a more auspicious metropolitan debut, and he seemed ready to take his place as a significant new talent in the international art world, finding himself much in demand, particularly as a portraitist, and able now to lease a studio in London (although he kept, and often returned to, the studio his father built for him at the family's new home, Morfydd House, 1120 Llangyfelach Road). But this early triumph proved something of a mirage: Walters failed to consolidate his position in the years after that exhibition, with his former admirers deserting him in bafflement the further he moved away from portraiture in favour of "extreme" or "freakish" experimentation. There was, for instance, undisguised hostility to his painting Annunciation (1933), which depicted the Angel Gabriel alighting from an aeroplane in full flying gear to be greeted by the Virgin Mary dressed in pyjamas. There would be four more London exhibitions between 1930 and 1948, but no reprise of the Warren Gallery success; indeed, at the Coolings Gallery in 1936, he failed to sell a single picture.

Unperturbed by the lack of commercial success, the determinedly professional Walters forged on — with a single-mindedness, indeed, which seems to have contributed to the collapse of his 1934 marriage, after only a few months, to Marjorie Davies, a tutor at Swansea School of Art (who, as Mrs Walters, continued to teach in Swansea's stained glass department until her retirement in the 1970s). Walters "found it difficult to adapt himself to the give and take of married life", suggested Erna Meinel, whom the painter met in 1936 and with whom he lived during his last years, after spending the 1938-46 period in Swansea.

It was in the early 1930s that he began, with paintings such as Annunciation, to stray from the styles that pleased his early supporters, having reached the conclusion that the camera had made naturalistic painting redundant. "The pictures in our Galleries appear as though the artists who painted them used only one eye instead of two," he wrote in 1936, when he was already deeply immersed in the development of his double vision or binocular technique. It arose from Walters' simple observation, while staring into the fire one evening, of two images of his foot when it was not directly in focus. His painting would endeavour thereafter to account for the way in which each eye records an object separately and from a slightly different viewpoint. The results could be bizarre — as in *A Study from Life* (1944), a self-portrait done apparently with his nose against a mirror (a position which nullifies normal binocular vision), in which the artist appears as a Hitler-like Cyclops, the earnest penetration of his gaze augmenting the (surely) unintended comedy of the piece. But when combined with techniques derived from his art school training, the binocular approach is capable of transcending the limitations of a semi-scientific exercise, resulting in powerfully affecting works of art. His colours, during these later years, became more vivid, and he often applied them in an Impressionistic sort of brickwork, building up vertical lines with hundreds of short, horizontal brushstrokes, and imbuing the best of his work with vibrant and richly variable rhythms. He also made much within his paintings of framing devices and motifs, including double-vision studies of empty picture frames. There are landscapes seen through open windows; there are paintings in which the actual subjects — such as *Girl in Kitchen* (c. 1938) and *Woman Reading* (c. 1937) — occupy only a fraction of the canvas, most of the surface being devoted to the doors, corridors and doorways that frame them. There is the unflinching *Artist's Mother Asleep* (c. 1937) — and seemingly close to death — framed by the unyielding metal bars of her bed, which contrast with the hallucinated, disproportionate bed-knobs hovering about her like spectral, promissory orbs.

The depth, complexity and shifting focus of the best of his binocular studies make for an art of profound humanity, as Walters, transcending both naturalism and theory, succeeds in rendering the essence of the scene or the moment. But few, in his lifetime, sympathized with what he was trying to achieve. "I wish Evan Walters had stuck to 'straight painting' as he called it and not gone off on to this double vision business," Mrs Coombe Tennant wrote to a friend in 1949. "I was really distressed when I saw what he had sent in to the National Society Show. Formless and frightfully ugly things." It was a view shared by many, including the Irish playwright Sean O'Casey (1880- 1964), who became a close friend of Walters after the Warren Gallery exhibition and who owned six of his paintings. Writing to her shortly after the painter's death, and addressing her as "My dear Mam o Nedd", O'Casey said, "I wish I could have kept close to Evan, for I imagine I had a steadying influence on him... I'm sure I could have laughed away his odd idea of double vision — such a waste of grand talent."

His final exhibition in London, at the Alpine Club Gallery in 1950, resulted in only a few sales, and friends noted a certain disenchantment in his manner at this juncture. One of them, paying Walters a visit, recorded the poignant scene of the artist asleep on the settle in an empty gallery. In spite of the exhibition's failure to re-establish his reputation, he would no doubt have been looking forward to a major exhibition of his work being planned at the Glynn Vivian; but he died in his London studio of a heart attack, aged 58, and the anticipated homecoming of the most successful artist that Swansea, at that time, had ever produced became the 1952 memorial exhibition.

His one, constant champion — until her death in 1977 — was Erna Meinel, the subject of several of his works, including the remarkable portrait *Lady in a Black Hat* (1938). She recognised that — like, for instance, Cezanne before him — he was attempting to evolve a genuinely innovatory vocabulary in paint, and that he was "the first artist, as far as we know, to draw and paint the appearance of objects as seen in indirect vision, and so to make the first known pictorial records of what double images look like to an artist... One is struck by the *familiarity* of the impressions conveyed and we feel, by use of transparent and opaque images, that he has given us the spirit of such scenes rather than a factual record."

It is to be hoped that over half a century since the artist's death, Erna Mienel's estimation of his continuous revolution is no longer held to be as partisan and eccentric as perhaps it formerly was, and that visitors to the Glynn Vivian this Eisteddfod time might discover that when putting his theories at the service of art, rather than his art at the service of his theories, Evan Walters was indeed capable of producing great pictures.

I would like to thank the staff of the Glynn Vivian Art Gallery, Swansea, in particular Jenni Spencer-Davies (Director), Ellie Dawkins and Evelyn Smith, for allowing me access to the gallery's Evan Walters holdings and to fascinating letters, articles and papers in the archive. I am grateful also to the art historian Barry Plummer, curator of the Glynn Vivian's retrospective exhibition and editor of a forthcoming book of paintings and drawings by Evan Walters, for much invaluable information about the artist's life and for kindly reading and commenting on an early draft of this article.

PLANET 178

Adrian Mitchell (1932-2008) and Wales

A memoir by Nigel Jenkins

"*Timor mortis conturbat me*" (fear of death disturbs me), the sobering Latin phrase[1] that tolls through many a late medieval poem, was the remorseless refrain of Adrian Mitchell's "Lament for the Welsh Makers", which he published in the Welsh fortnightly *Arcade* on 12 December, 1980. As the magazine went to press, John Lennon was assassinated in New York , and Adrian sent me a letter shortly afterwards containing an impromptu coda to his "Lament":

> *Gentle-tough Lennon, where's he gone?*
> *Brian only knows — but his love flies on,*
> *Its wings beat beatifically —*
> *The fear of death moves inside me.*

Adrian, who had been undertaking a fellowship at Cambridge, wrote that he had been "absolutely messed up into bloody ribbons by John Lennon's death. I have been listening to his songs every night while alone in Cambridge on this Fellowship. He was the best we had."

As news broke of Adrian's own unexpected death on 20 December, 2008 — from heart failure, following a bout of pneumonia from which he had seemed to be recovering — there must have been many like me, all over the world, who found themselves similarly "messed up into ribbons" and drinking away benumbed and disbelieving midnights with a book of Adrian's poems in hand. Rereading the numerous letters he'd sent me over the years, which I'd filed haphazardly among the pages of his collections, it seemed almost unimaginable that such a huge-hearted and life-enhancing spirit had been so peremptorily snuffed — for despite his seventy-six years he had the passion, energy and unabashed "optimism of the will" of a man less than half his age. I miss him, of course, as a dear friend, but he was one of those exceptional beings — like John Lennon — whose loss may be felt with a rare intensity even by those who never knew him in person: his writings — tender, angry, clear, direct, disarmingly honest, playful, fantastical and utterly uninterested in dishing up for the critics the fashionable clever-dickery that seems to be the *raison d'être* of too much contemporary verse — forged a conduit of mutually intimate rapport between himself and his readers and listeners, of all ages and conditions. He meant more to more people than just about any other poet in the countries of Britain, and it was gratifying to see it acknowledged in the *Guardian* that of the three substantial figures of the British left who died within days of each other — Adrian Mitchell, Harold Pinter and Bernard Crick — "in terms of spreading good values, getting people to laugh and feel angry for the right reasons, it may be that Mitchell mattered most."[2]

Adrian's debut collection, *Poems* (Cape, 1964), was probably the first book of poetry I ever bought, aged about fifteen, and he has been a bedrock bardic companion ever since (although we didn't actually meet for another fifteen years). I was buying records by the Beatles, the Rolling Stones, the Pretty Things, Bob Dylan — and Adrian Mitchell, though older and much more (then) of a jazzer than I was, appealed to me as unmistakably a part of the counter-culture that was vibrantly in the making: the exuberance, iconoclasm, irreverence, anarchic humour and angry protest that I relished in the music of the '60s I also found abundantly active in this subversive new poetry. As Mike Horovitz would later comment, Adrian Mitchell "simply snarls for real decency, intelligence, imagination".[3] Some of his material has dated, of course, as has much of the referential political satire of, say, the eighteenth century: a young reader today would no doubt need footnotes for topics such as Suez, Lord Home and Pal Meat for Dogs. But it holds its own as a valuable record of the times, while other pieces will have work to do for as long as we have war, starvation, monarchy, greed, exploitation, -isms of all destructive shades, love, children, music, pleasure, life and death.

One notably enduring poem from that era, his most famous, is "To Whom It May Concern", a rhythm-and-blues incantation against war and the ways in which we gladly collude with the media and consumerism to shield ourselves from its horrors. With its insistent refrain, "Tell me lies about Vietnam", the poem was first performed at the anti-Vietnam War protest in Trafalgar Square in 1964, and it electrified thousands at the historic Poetry Olympics at the Albert Hall in 1965;[4] this performance marked a major breakthrough, which ensured a popular reception for just about everything Adrian subsequently published or staged. He read the poem hundreds of times since then, often changing "Vietnam" to whatever wars may have been disfiguring the planet at the time. "Tell me lies about Iraq" he'd latterly chorus, and had he been with us in Castle Square, Swansea in January 2009 he'd have done as the reader of his poem did on that desperate occasion and intone "Tell me lies about Gaza".

It's difficult to think of a more captivating performer of poetry than Adrian. I saw him "live" for the first time c.1970 in the hangar-like gymnasium of Lanchester Polytechnic in Coventry, where a day-long poetry marathon was being held, as part of the Lanchester Arts Festival. The event attracted thousands, and all of the poets involved — among them Seamus Heaney, John Montague, Brian Patten, Roger McGough, Christopher Logue — relied gratefully on the PA system to deliver their words. But not Adrian, who strode to the microphone — and switched it off, confident that his unamplified voice, its music in league with his body's movement, would communicate the message, and trusting that having established aural parity with his audience he would be more receptive to their responses, even to the extent, as he used to say, of hearing something of what they were thinking. Never losing sight of poetry's origins in music and dance, he tried in his readings to reunite these elements, using all the rhythms, intonations and physical gestures that were available to him, and improvising wherever possible. He was skilled at varying the pace and tone of a reading, alternating, for instance, the high seriousness of an angry celebration of the Chilean folk-singer Victor Jara, murdered by the fascist junta in 1973, with, say, the absurd knockabout of a poem such as "Ten ways to avoid lending your wheelbarrow to anyone" (i.e. the lecherous gambit: "May I borrow your wheelbarrow?" "Only if I can fuck your wife in it."). There were, of course, many occasions on which he was obliged to use the microphone, such as large peace rallies or the huge anti-monarchist People's Jubilee organised by the Communist Party at the Alexandra Palace in north London in 1977. But whether addressing a roomful of school children or 90,000 people in Hyde Park, his readings were invariably an irresistible combination of energy and intimacy, the primal "hear me talkin to ya" cry of blues and jazz.

Adrian's "Welsh connection" begins with his wife Celia, who stars — sometimes lustily — in many of his poems. Born Celia Hewitt in Hawarden, Flintshire, in 1933, she was an actor working for Kenneth Tynan on the ITV arts programme *Tempo* when she and Adrian met in the early 1960s. "My wife is Welsh," he wrote to me in the early days of our correspondence, "she sings it though she doesn't speak it." For the five decades that followed, Celia was Adrian's anchor and inspiration.

Between 1974 and 1975, Adrian was writer-in-residence at the Sherman Theatre, Cardiff. It was, I think, around this time that the Welfare State Theatre Company asked Adrian to write some song lyrics for a show to be staged in Caerffili Castle; the project ran into funding difficulties and was abandoned, but not before Adrian had researched and written a fair amount of material. I first caught wind of this project in a letter he sent me in 1980:

Best wishes to Gweithdŷ Barddoniaeth Abertawe[5] in the names of Aneirin, Taliesin, Llywarch and his 24 sons, Myrddin, Gwalchmai, Hywel, Dafydd ap Gwilym, Gwerful Mechain, Gruffudd Gryg, Llywelyn Goch, Gwerful Madog, Dafydd ab Edmwnd, Lewys Môn, Siôn Tudur, Dic Huws and Dylan Thomas. When I come to Swansea I'll read my "Lament for the Welsh Makers" — or better still my Welsh wife will.

Intrigued that this London-based poet, strongly associated with the English Left, had immersed himself to this extent in the barddas[6] of Wales, I asked to see the poem, imagining that it would be likely to appeal to the readers of Arcade, which I was helping to edit. Along came the "Lament", with a letter explaining more of the background:

The plot involved finding out a lot about Welsh literature, particularly poetry. Although my wife is Welsh […] my knowledge is very slight. So I read the books, or as many as I could in the brief time I had, I read the poets in translation and read the stories of their lives and, for all my ignorance, I was moved.

How to live your life as a poet, and how to die your death — these are very particular problems. I decided to borrow the structure of William Dunbar's great Lament for the Makars and to set into it hints of the lives of the Welsh bards. I felt and still feel tentative. Would this be seen as yet another example of the crushing colonial Brit on the steal, the white man making another take-over bid for jazz? I hope not. It is meant to be, in the main, a homage. I do love

Wales and I wanted to express some of that love.

The poem, comprising twenty-seven four-line line stanzas, is a dignified danse macabre in the emotionally stark register of the Scottish model. It begins:

WILLIAM DUNBAR sang piteously
When he mourned for the Makers of poetry.
He engraved their names with this commentary —
Timor mortis conturbat me.

DUNBAR, I'm Scot-begotten too,
But I would celebrate a few
Welsh masters of the wizardry —
The fear of death moves inside me.

And it concludes:

The black lungs swell, the black harp sighs,
Whenever a Welsh maker dies.
Forgive my nervous balladry —
Timor mortis conturbat me.

I had asked him to comment, for *Arcade*'s readers, on his own sense of nationhood. "I don't have a nation," he wrote: My father was a Scot but he moved to England for the War and the work. I feel no more alien in Wales than I do in England or Scotland or the USA. What am I getting defensive about? Because I'm aware of the Nationalist movement in Wales and support its aims — as a stage along the devolutionary road away from nationhood, towards something on a much smaller and more human scale.

(Adrian felt passionately — and nowhere more so than in the field of education — that "small is beautiful". He argued at every opportunity that if the number of pupils per class could be reduced radically to around a dozen, life in these islands would be transformed.)

Well known in and familiar with Cardiff from 1974 onwards, Adrian did not read in Swansea until 1981. Once or twice a year, I'd be asked by Pontardawe Folk Club to book them a poet. Agreeing to perform at Pontardawe, Adrian asked me to fix him up with a school reading as well — to make the journey from London worthwhile. "How many kids do you want to read to?" I asked him. "As many as you like," he said, "fill the hall." I took him at his word and made the necessary arrangements at Olchfa Comprehensive School in "posh" Swansea west. The event is remembered in a horror poem entitled "The Olchfa Reading" and beginning "I had told Nigel Jenkins/the bard of Mumbles, who was my friend,/that I wanted to read to a large audience..." (note that "was"). The poem goes on to describe his encounter "in a hall the size of/a Jumbo Jet hanger" with a crowd "as multitudinous/as the armies of Genghis Khan/but they were larger and hairier/and less interested in poetry". Well, at least Adrian got a poem out of it — one of his comic masterpieces, indeed. A packed and appreciative house at the Dynevor Arms in Pontardawe that night more than made up for his Olchfa nightmare.

It was probably on the occasion of this visit that I took him down to Laugharne for the first time, to see Dylan Thomas's grave and his writing shed, and to visit the Boathouse and Brown's Hotel. Long before his appointment as Dylan Thomas Fellow in the UK Year of Literature and Writing 1995, Adrian was a huge fan of Swansea's self-declared "Rimbaud of Cwmdonkin Drive". In June 1982, he phoned to ask if he and his friend Jeremy Brooks — who, as literary manager of the Royal Shakespeare Company in the 1960s, had worked with Adrian on a renowned adaptation of Peter Weiss's

Marat/Sade (1964) and the collectively authored *US* (1966) — could come and stay for a few days, as they had been commissioned to devise a stage version of Dylan Thomas's autobiographical story 'A Child's Christmas in Wales', and wanted to get seriously to grips with "the matter of Swansea".

So over they came, to the leaky asbestos shack in Mumbles, with its expansive view of Swansea Bay, which I shared with my then partner, the harpist and actress Delyth Evans (who would later perform in the British premiere of *A Child's Christmas*). Their stay amounted to one long, delightful party, but we managed, nevertheless, to get some purposeful research done: Dylan Thomas's birthplace at 5 Cwmdonkin Drive; Cwmdonkin Park; the Uplands Hotel (now Tavern), just before (I think) its grotesque make-over as The Street; the No Sign wine-bar in Wind Street; sewin and chips in the Queen's Hotel in Gloucester Place; Pantycelyn Road in Townhill, to get a sense of the lie of Swansea's land, and to explore the possibility for their play of some class warfare, in the park below, between the Townhill boys and the Uplands boys. I spouted forth, the playwrights took copious notes, and Adrian the (very) amateur photographer snapped away with his 'camera for fools'.

Most of us have been browbeaten, by the time we reach adulthood, into "putting away childish things", but Adrian never lost sight of the child within. He had, as Ted Hughes observed, "the innocence of his own experience", and he brought to *A Child's Christmas in Wales* the irrepressible playfulness and inventiveness that characterise his many poems and plays for children. He loved games, and it was on this visit that he introduced us to the *High Noon* hilarity of the England's Glory "shoot-out": the two "gunmen", with their weapons — a box of matches apiece — in their trouser pockets, stand back-to-back; then, on the command "Walk!", they take six paces forward, turn, and fire, whereupon they whip out their matchboxes, fumble forth a match — and strike it, the first to strike a light being the victor. On subsequent visits, he'd whoop away many an hour playing with our small daughters, Angharad and Branwen, on their mini pinball machine, requesting yet more Chuck Berry as soundtrack for the threesome's anarchy.

Jeremy Brooks (1926—1994) too was splendid company. He'd been educated in Llandudno and had lived near Llanfrothen, Gwynedd, since 1953, with a base also in London (one of his four novels, *Jampot Smith* [1960], was republished in Parthian's Library of Wales series in 2008). He knew the north well, but, like Adrian, was less familiar with the south, and Swansea in particular. They had a tight deadline, the world premiere of their "play with songs" having been scheduled for December 1982 — six months after their research trip to Swansea — at the Ohio Theatre, Cleveland; the company had stipulated that it wanted a first draft by the end of August and a final draft by mid October. After their departure for what Adrian called "Jeremy's garden of Eden" in Gwynedd, to work intensively on the first draft, there was a flurry of correspondence between us. They wanted more Swansea slang: I gave them things such as "wuss", "twp", "twpsin", "cowin lush" (which Adrian loved), and other ideas for "brushing colours into the script". They wanted rough recordings of "Calon Lân" and "Sospan Fach" (for a mock rugby match between Dylan and uncles, with a cushion for a ball). They wanted a general pronunciation crib, feedback on maps they'd made, and responses to certain scenes or characters they were experimenting with. There were regular progress reports:

Jeremy and I had a good session yesterday with the aid of multitudinous photos and maps of the park and seashore which Jeremy made. We are probably going to use maps (seagull's eye view like the seashore one) as backdrops for the two outdoor scenes. Jeremy will write the park, I'll write the seashore. The hunchback will be seen but not, I think, heard. We are working on the characters of uncles and aunts, deepening them, giving them more sense of social background. We are giving one of them the kind of fanaticism for socialism and rugby which I remember from long sessions in Llanelli pubs. So the dreaded word [socialism] will be heard in Cleveland, Ohio.

....

I think it's developing well. Trouble is, we've got far too much material and it's probably half an hour too long at the moment. You shall see it later when we do the second draft — there'll still be plenty of time to change things. I'm sure it's not Christmas-cardy or quaint. And I think it takes place in a real town of imaginative people.

Inventive as their writing was, in order to turn Dylan Thomas's words for the page into engaging drama, they were concerned, as Adrian wrote, to "use considerable narration, direct to audience, from the original. Don't like to waste a drop of it."

In mid October, they sent me the fourth draft for checking, after which everything was in the hands of the director, Clifford Williams, and the American cast. The play was well received by audiences and critics, the show-biz magazine *Variety* declaring "the show has the qualities to become a holiday classic". Having somewhat muted the show's Welshness for American audiences (and removed terms such as "sugar fags"), the dramatists were keen, in Jeremy's words, to see it produced "Welshly in Wales". This was realised in October/November 1984, when it was produced at the Torch Theatre, Milford Haven. This highly acclaimed British premiere established *A Child's Christmas in Wales* as a seasonal staple on this side of the Atlantic too.

The show's traditional and freshly minted songs were a significant presence, as music has been in most of Adrian's plays; the influence of music — above all, jazz and blues — has also determined the form and feel of much of his poetry. He was a natural choice, therefore, as speaker and performer — in league with his sometime collaborator the composer Pete Moser — when the Welsh Union of Writers held its 1986 annual conference, at Clyne Castle, Swansea, on the theme of "Words and Music". Other key contributors that weekend were the opera-singer Sir Geraint Evans, the folk-singer Frankie Armstrong, the poet, short-story writer Glyn Jones and the critic M. Wynn Thomas, who spoke on "Prison and Hotel — Two Images of Contemporary Wales". "I enjoyed Wynn Thomas, mostly, and Frankie Armstrong entirely," Adrian later wrote to me. "I have just about got over my awe of Frankie because she's got such a sense of humour and loves a giggle... good to be among so many familiar friendly faces." Two somewhat dour faces at Clyne belonged to a pair of sober-suited members of the Soviet Writers Union who had somehow wangled an invitation to the conference. Participants spent the weekend trying to work out whether the men from Moscow were defecting, spying — or both. But Adrian was more exercised by the unwelcome antics of a television crew who had been sent to film the proceedings. "Oh those telly fools," he later wrote to me:

...they couldn't film anything that existed, they had to rearrange people and objects. I was astonished that they didn't issue us with special clothes and bully us into putting them on. I think they deserve a beady-eyed poem from someone. The kitchen staff were darlings and if the TV people were rude to them they are even worse clods than I thought.

While regretting having had insufficient time to prepare and present his contribution with Pete Moser, Adrian said he considered song to be "the most popular form of artistic communication and writers ought to treat it seriously." When Tŷ Newydd, the National Writers' Centre for Wales in Llanystumdwy near Cricieth, opened in the early 1990s, Mitchell and Moser were able to give song-writing the attention it deserved, in a week-long course — the first of many courses tutored by Adrian at Tŷ Newydd. He was, of course, an exceptionally gifted and stimulating teacher, for learners of all ages, just as he was unusually supportive of fellow writers: you'd get a phone call out of the blue — "Loved that poem of yours in [such-and-such a publication]" — which would make your day.

His experiences as Dylan Thomas Fellow at the UK Year of Literature and Writing 1995 — the Swansea-centred and self-styled "biggest festival of literature the world has ever seen" — are crystallised in the jumbo-sized *Who Killed Dylan Thomas* which he published, with exuberantly anarchic illustrations by his friend Ralph Steadman, in 1998. The Year of Literature, one of a series of government-sponsored, year-long festivals, in which selected British cities celebrated a chosen art form, brought many of the world's greatest wordsmiths to Swansea: Allen Ginsberg, Seamus Heaney, Denise Levertov, Sorley MacLean, Yehuda Amichai, Miroslav Holub, Kenzaburo Oe, Rita Dove, Amos Oz, Irena Ratushinskaya, Michael Ondaatje, John Berger, Van Morrison, R.S. Thomas — to name only a tiny fraction. In a piece entitled "Thanks for the fellowship", Adrian wrote:

As Dylan Thomas Fellow
I've enjoyed myself greatly.
I've stayed in a friendly hotel with fantail doves
eating digestive biscuits on my windowsill
and friendly dogs for breakfast.

I've been to many readings, performances and mumbles
by visiting writers from misunderstood countries,
I've chatted with them, eaten with them,
bought some of their books and showed them the delights

of Salubrious Passage, my favourite ghostwalk,
under which I heard the Italian Love Gods play.

The "argument" of this roller-coaster of a book is that Dylan Thomas was killed not by any individual (including himself) but by the miserliness of cultural institutions and the insouciance of home audiences who had failed to value their poet. Towards the end of the book, he urges his readers: "Put your money where your heart is":

If you get a fine new arts centre like this one [i.e. the Dylan Thomas Centre] — hang on to it. There are always faceless businessmen lurking to plan to turn any beautiful building into a Conference Centre in which to play a faceless future. Watch out for them, fight them off, hold on to your good space, hang on Sloopy.
Do not let your love for Dylan Thomas and his poems overshadow or overwhelm your love for the hundreds of good poets still at work in the world — the poets of Swansea and Wales both in Welsh and English — and the poets of the world.

Several of the Swansea poems Adrian wrote during the fellowship — among them "Swansea Triplets", "Night Thoughts in Swansea", "In the Queen's Hotel, Swansea" and "Night Thoughts in Treorchy" — appear in his 1996 collection *Blue Coffee. Who Killed Dylan Thomas* — from the Dylan Thomas Centre's own press, Tŷ Llên Publications — was launched at the first-ever Dylan Thomas Festival in 1998. Both Adrian and Ralph were in notably festive spirits as the launch got under way, and there was much hilarity during their reading-cum-slide-show as the synchronisation of word and image became increasingly wayward. At the signing afterwards, Ralph treated each buyer of the book to a caricature of Dylan on the title page, done in biro, red wine and brandy, while Adrian cartooned for everyone what looked like a cheery cross between the Labrador's head and the elephant which — generally singly — he would characteristically inscribe in books and letters.

It was back, then, to Adrian's "friendly hotel with fantail doves", the Windsor Lodge, near the bottom of Mount Pleasant, where Dylan Thomas's daughter Aeronwy, Ralph, Adrian and friends were stood a meal by festival director Dave Woolley. While the rest of us were content with the house red, Ralph — who can afford to like good wine — ordered for himself, at his own expense, a £100 bottle of the best red in the cellar. During the meal, Ralph doodled — again, in biro, red wine and brandy — a caricature of Aeronwy on his cloth napkin, an angular, if hardly flattering, likeness. Then he ordered a second £100-bottle of wine and, to the waitress's confusion, offered to pay for it with the hotel's own napkin on which he'd been scribbling. The owner was called, but she had no hesitation in exchanging that bottle of wine for an original Ralph Steadman.

Adrian missed out on the meal, having floated aloft on a cloud of Hippocrene. As a performer of impeccable poise and timing, he was always careful with the booze before a reading. But afterwards, like many of us, he'd often gear up into celebration mode — a tendency he acknowledges in "Poetry readings", published in *Who Killed Dylan Thomas*:

After a reading
if the poet feels he has triumphed —
and poets mostly do, whatever the evidence —
the poet will want to celebrate by drinking himself
off the edge of the known world
I'm not defending this after-reading state,
which lasts around an hour,
I'm just describing it

and saying that it happens
and that it can be dangerous,
for if this white hour is disrupted
then the Oblivion Hunt will be on.

We read together at Theatr Hafren, Newtown during the 1996 Mid Wales May Festival. The "water" Adrian had been drinking beforehand turned miraculously into vodka as we left the stage, and it wasn't long before we two wobblers needed a taxi back to our hotel, the Elephant and Castle. I saw him safely to his room, assuming a restful night thereafter would be had by all. But, as recounted at breakfast, Adrian had a nocturnal adventure. Waking after a while to take a pee, he had let himself into what he thought was his en suite bathroom, but the door he'd found was the door into the corridor — which had slammed behind him, locked fast against re-entry. The naked and toothless midnight rambler, busting for a pee, had searched on all floors for a bathroom or a toilet, getting more and more lost and more and more desperate for that waz. Eventually, he'd found his way down to the lobby where he'd been rescued from his bladder-wracked plight by a startled night-porter.

One of the many things that Adrian gave Wales (and the world) was England, or a version of England — Tom Paine's, William Blake's, Byron's, Shelley's, John Berger's, an England of peace demos, rock and pop music, subversive and wacky humour, internationalism, incipient socialism and republicanism, unabashed sexuality, resourcefulness, invention and vision — with which the non-English, especially England's frequently disdained Celtic neighbours, could feel comfortable. He may often have claimed that he had no nation, but his poetry shows him to have been an English patriot — of the most constructive and beneficial kind. The institutions and practices he attacks are attacked, generally, according to the part they play in holding England and her people back from true fulfilment. In his tongue-in-cheek poem of national origins, "Ancestors", he describes the early English people as a "Hairy red story-telling, song-singing, dragon-fighting, fire-drinking tribe" who were subdued by rapacious invaders who grabbed their land and imposed an alien form of class society on them: "It was robbery with most bloody violence." But elsewhere, he is confident that beneath the disfiguring scab of Capitalism and imperial decline there resides a regenerative energy capable of transforming the political landscape:

> For underneath the welded Carnaby
> Spike-studded dog-collar groincrusher boots,
> Blood-coloured combinations
> And the golfing socks which stink of Suez,
> Underneath the Rolls Royce heart
> Worn on a sleeve encrusted with royal snot,
> Underneath the military straitjacket
> From the Dead Meat Boutique —
> > Lives
> > A body
> Of incredibly green beauty.

— that last line consciously echoing the "green and pleasant land" of William Blake's great hymn to an England re-imagined. That this patriot for all that is best and potential in England has been so popular in Wales also — not least among those poets characterised by Tony Conran as the "Idrisiaid", namely the socialist, republican, nationalist and internationalist literary sons and daughters of the poet Idris Davies — is hardly surprising. Adrian Mitchell gives us a poetry, a politics and an England with which we can happily make common cause.

In several poems, Adrian faced unflinchingly the prospect of his own death. One of two epitaphs he wrote for himself reads simply: "I stopped living/but kept on loving".[7] His poetry will continue to do what it has always done: making the world a better place.

PLANET EXTRA 29 DECEMBER 2008

1. From a responsory of the Catholic Office of the Dead, in the third Nocturn of Matins.
2. "In terms of spreading values, Mitchell mattered most", by Jackie Ashley, in the *Guardian*, 29 December 2008.
3. Mike Horovitz, in his introduction to *Children of Albion: Poetry of the Underground in Britain*, Penguin Books, 1969.
4. A clip of Adrian Mitchell reading the poem at the Albert Hall, and more recently, may be seen on the Bloodaxe website,
   http://www.bloodaxebooks.com/titlepage.asp?isbn=1852248432
5. Swansea Poetry Workshop, a now defunct poetry publishing co-operative of which I was secretary.
6. Bardic lore.
7 "Alternative Selfepitaph", *All Shook Up: Poems 1997-2000*, Bloodaxe Books, 2000.

Batting for Essex, England
— and the World

Nigel Jenkins on the English poet David Cobb

After David Cobb had been awarded his first prize in the 1991 Cardiff International Haiku Competition, in a ceremony at St David's Hall, I — as co-judge (with David Kerrigan) — taxied him up to the BBC in Llandaff to record an interview for Radio Four's *Kaleidoscope*. Having asked him a few general questions, the presenter duly invited Mr Cobb to read his winning poem. He obliged:

within the shadow
of the blossoming tree
my shadow

There followed a slightly awkward silence. "Is that... all?" she enquired, implying that £500 was a mighty prize for so few words. Although this was an arts programme, the presenter evidently had no idea what to expect of a haiku. Her perplexity was probably less of a surprise to Cobb than was, to her, the disarming brevity of his poem, such was — and is — the ignorance that prevails about this most concise of verse forms, which originated in Japan about four hundred years ago and began to make its faltering way westward around the beginning of the twentieth century. Even those who pretend to an interest in the form are capable of misconstruing it. When the *New Welsh Review* published a selection of the competition's winning and commended entries, the professors of poultry were quick to complain that Kerrigan and I, having favoured many haiku that — like Cobb's — "failed" to add up to the "requisite" seventeen syllables, were obviously innumerate incompetents. One, indeed, accused us of being in the pay of the Americans, whose flouting of the "rule" that there be five syllables in the first line, seven in the second and five in the third, he deemed to be responsible for the haiku's impending ruination. If, in recent years, it has become better understood among practitioners that twelve to fourteen syllables of English are "sufficient" in the way that seventeen *onji* are sufficient for the purposes of haiku in Japanese (and "sufficiency" is, of course, a desirable mark of the best haiku), it is still the case that most dabblers in haiku fail to appreciate that there is very much more to it than mere elegance of form. Many three-liners masquerading as haiku in the collections of "mainstream" poets (as haikuists call those who write in generally longer forms) constitute what may be regarded, in effect, as a new form of poetry — the five-seven-fiver; they are rarely haiku, often because form seems to be the writer's preoccupation.

Other "foreign" forms, such as the sonnet and the villanelle, long ago established themselves in English and other languages, and have developed distinctive native identities outside their countries of origin, but the haiku and its associated forms — the senryu, the tanka, the haibun — continue to struggle for recognition as serious contenders. While various "mainstream" poets are busy muddying the haiku pond with their half-baked five-seven-fivery, others are to be found loftily dismissing the form as some effete, alien irrelevance, the sad pursuit of anoraks and frog-spotters.

If haiku and haibun enjoyed the respect accorded to other naturalised literary forms, David Cobb would be published by a major English publisher and celebrated as one of England's finest contemporary writers, with double-page profiles in the weekend supplements to prove it. But haiku is in its infancy in Britain, haibun is virtually unheard of, and members of an insular and incurious literary establishment would seem to lack the innocence and humility needed to appreciate these forms. Two hundred years ago they might have overlooked the strengths of William Blake. Perhaps part of the trouble is that, as R.H. Blyth observed, "The nature of haiku cannot be rightly understood until it is realised that they imply a revolution in our everyday life and ways of thinking." It's true that many inadequate haiku find their way into public view, especially on the web. Frequently cited flaws include a predictable "sameness", a superficial imagism lacking resonance and depth, pseudo-Zen whimsicalities, heavy-handed symbolism, carelessness in the orchestration of language, and what the poet Jackie Hardy, when she tired of editing the haiku magazine *Blithe Spirit*, characterised as the "rhapsodic musings of middle-class escapists". But to dismiss an entire genre on the basis of the shortcomings of its lesser practitioners — as many outside the haiku kraal seem wont to do — is as myopic as consigning, say, the rhyming couplet to the bin of literary history because you have read only the treasurable effusions of William McGonagall, and have yet to discover Alexander Pope. Although not the sort to bear grudges, Cobb has noted over the years representative instances of "mainstream" coolness towards haiku: Peter Forbes, during his editorship of *Poetry Review*, writing to Cobb that he was "not very keen on haiku", failing to review a single haiku volume and carrying a review of Paul Muldoon's *Hay* that made no mention of that book's ninety haiku; Craig Raine, when editor at Faber, declaring haiku of "limited if genuine interest"; Michael Schmidt, of Carcanet, admitting to Cobb that he couldn't stomach haiku because he was "strongly prejudiced against form" of any kind; Neil Astley, of Bloodaxe Books, admiring Cobb's haiku yet deciding that they "would not suit his list"; the poet laureate, Andrew Motion, writing to Cobb that reading haiku at length had "a rather wearying effect" (why should Motion feel he has to read them at length?); Sean O'Brien, in *Northern Review*, declaring that the pioneering anthology *The Iron Book of British Haiku* (eds., David Cobb and Martin Lucas, Iron Press, 1998) would "find an honoured place in many lavatories"; and the literary press in general ignoring the form — no mention, for instance, in the *Times Literary Supplement* and its ilk of *The Haiku Hundred* (eds., James Kirkup, David Cobb and Peter Mortimer; Iron Press, 1992), which has sold over 9000 copies (compared with the few hundred that is the lot of most slim volumes reviewed by the *TLS*).

This lack of acceptance does not worry every haikuist (some of whom can be as wilfully ignorant of "mainstream" poetry as many "mainstream" poets are of haiku), but it worries Cobb. "I don't want to appear as an outsider in my own land, [imitating] some foreign literary form," he told the Japanese magazine *Yusei* in 2003. "I want haiku to become, with necessary adaptations, a part of the total English literary scene. To do that, haiku has to overcome a 'bad press'. It is still too often rejected because people, who really don't know much about it, think of it as genteel, predictable, not proactive enough and, in short, irrelevant to our problem-ridden times." Both as a practitioner and as a resourceful campaigner, Cobb has been at the centre of a resurgence of interest in haiku in the countries of Britain, and he has played a seminal role in the introduction and development of the haibun. He is recognised among aficionados worldwide, to quote the Welsh haikuist Ken Jones, as "the Grand Old Man of British haiku" — although he was a late starter, publishing his first poetry in 1989 at the age of 63.

The son of a clerk on the LMS Railway, David Cobb was born (1926) and raised a few miles north of London, where the urban and the rural intermingled and where he developed a passion for cricket (when he retired from the game in 2001, he had played in about twelve hundred matches). His youth was dominated by nearly four years of national service as a trooper with the Life Guards, during which he saw Germany, Egypt and Palestine, experience which no doubt contributed to this English patriot's resolutely internationalist outlook. He studied German at Bristol University,

128

anticipating a working life as a grammar school teacher, but then found himself taking other directions: with Unesco to Hamburg; with the British Council to Bangkok; eventually, on the staff of an international publishing house, to many other countries in Europe, the Middle East and Africa, as an author and adviser in the field of English as a foreign or second language. (His long intimacy with the English language, particularly his palpable enthusiasm for its Germanic registers, contributes to the distinctive muscularity of his poetry.) Widowed twice and divorced twice, he has five children, and has lived since 1973 in Essex.

Cobb's interest in haiku began in 1977 when he was researching how English was being taught in Japanese high schools. He was rescued from his hit-and-miss initial flounderings by Joan Giroux's useful guide for the beginner, *The Haiku Form* (1974); the example of certain American poets helped, and there were the voluminous reflections on Japanese poetry by his fellow Essexian R.H. Blyth, a selection of whose writings Cobb would later co-edit (with Stephen H. Gill) as *The Genius of Haiku* (1994). Many of the American Beats and their followers had been writing haiku since the 1950s, but there seemed to Cobb, as he persevered with his haiku apprenticeship, very little such activity in Britain — although there was probably more of it than he realised at the time. A haiku contest run by *The Guardian* in 1967 had attracted no fewer than 3000 entries, including some in Welsh, and in the 1970s and 1980s there were both "mainstream" poets (Tony Conran, Anthony Thwaite, James Kirkup, Chris Torrance) and haiku specialists (Bill Wyatt, Gerry Loose) to be found publishing haiku, if you knew where to look. Cobb's sense of isolation led him, with Dee Evetts, towards the foundation of the British Haiku Society (BHS). Launched formally in 1990, it has had a hugely beneficial impact on the development of the haiku, and Cobb, as a tireless activist and BHS president (1997-2002) has played a major ambassadorial role on the haiku's behalf — by, for instance, speaking at conferences at home and abroad, adjudicating contests, editing important publications, including the beautifully produced British Museum collection *Haiku* (2002), preparing a haiku starter-pack for schools, and organising an international England-to-France-and-back poetry jaunt on Le Shuttle, which was no doubt the first occasion on which a large number of poets had gathered to write haiku "under the sea".

It is, though, as a writer of some of the most resonant haiku to have been composed in English, and as initiator of the haibun in Britain, that David Cobb has made his most significant contribution — a contribution acknowledged by the many international prizes awarded him. The term haibun, which may be found as yet in no English dictionary of literary terms, will be strange to most readers; but anyone who has enjoyed the frequently reprinted Penguin Classic *The Narrow Road to the Deep North and Other Travel Sketches* by Matsuo Basho (1644-94) will have been reading haibun, which may be described as a fusion of haiku and haiku-like prose. Ranging in length from a handful of words ending with a haiku, to thousands of words with a number of haiku embedded at intervals, haibun may embrace description, narration, exposition, recollection, introspection and fantasy. The essential feature is a synergistic, non-illustrational relationship between the prose and the haiku. According to Ken Jones, pioneer of the haibun in Wales, the prose should be written in a concrete, economical, direct style, free from abstraction and philosophising; it should be crisp, light-handed and rich in imagery. The haiku and prose elements should form an organic whole, saying more together than either says on its own; at the same time, paradoxically, both should be able to pass the "stand alone" test. Although haibun writing fell out of favour in Japan over a century ago, its potential began, in the 1990s, to excite western haikuists, including Cobb.

He aimed high — and hit triumphantly home — with his first

major haibun excursion, *The Spring Journey to the Saxon Shore* (1997) which, at 8000 words, is comparable in length to Basho-'s *The Narrow Road to the Deep North*. It describes a 130-mile bicycle ride from his home in Shalford, Essex to the Norfolk coast, and is among the most democratic, warm-spirited and appealing explorations of England and Englishness(es) that I have encountered. The investigation is continued in the similarly impressive extended haibun "A Day in Twilight" and in various shorter pieces that appear in his collection *Palm* (2002) which, as virtually a selected poems, is probably the most comprehensive introduction to his work.

Dog roses, sextons, maypoles, summer fêtes, pheasant shoots and nine-men's morris — certain aspects of David Cobb's England might seem, from a distance, uncomfortably close to John Major's clichéd summary of middle England as warm beer, village cricket and old maids cycling to holy communion through the morning mist. Although such features may be part of picture-book, traditional England, they are, nevertheless, not mere figments of the romanticising imagination and they remain worthy of record, if not celebration; but they are by no means representative, in Cobb's writing, of the bigger, more complex picture. The England to which he attends, in the Simone Weil sense of a compelling particularity of vision founded on vigilant "looking", is also an England (not, in such respects, unlike Wales) of factory farms, electricity pylons, mobile phones, CCTV, holidays in Florida, "Thai Food All Day" — and profound mulchings of history, official and unofficial, which he, as a poet, is moved to nurture, no matter how totally some of his people seem to have forgotten themselves:

Outside the War Memorial Institute in North Creake asking directions to the Blood Gate. "You know, where the Saxons piled up their dead as a barricade against the Danes?" Heads shaken. Saxons?

Danes? Have I asked in South *Creake, maybe? In South Creake, "Did* *you enquire in* North *Creake?" No written signs to advise one, only* Stop me and buy one *on an old ice-cream tricycle outside a teashop...*

While many haibun writers are content to proceed along what Cobb calls the horizontal axis, which is to say depictions of present action, he is committed to introducing the vertical axis, the presence of the past, into many of his haibun, thereby conjuring up legendary or historical or invented characters, such as Boudica (Cobb is piously alert to the Celtic past and to remnants in his *bro* of the Welsh language), Edmund "our first patron saint, martyr, king of the East Angles" or, for example, a flint knapper:

At Grime's Graves, a man of uncertain age, straggly bearded, in a *dirty tunic. From a large pockmarked nodule of flint clenched between* *heel of hand and padded knee he chips out an axehead. In the* *language of their trade flint knappers are said to preserve the last few* *Stone Age words. No worksong on his lips. Songs as he might sing* *might give away his descent from Grim, Grime, Grimp, Odin,* *bush-bearded ubiquitous boy, stealer of migrant souls, for whom* *every dyke, ditch, mineshaft or large hole in the ground is to be named* *by the credulous, and wrapped in ballads, as ancient purposes lapse* *out of our memories.*

Cobb's engagement with the vertical axis stems from his personal philosophy — "a pretty half-baked one, I grant you" — which is that "I see my own life as an extension of the lives of my ancestors, and a link between their lives and the lives of my descendants." On his way to the Saxon shore he praises, in informed detail, the wild flowers along the way, and bends his knee to the dandelion: "Twenty-five generations of my family have done the same; and you were already old, old, very old indeed, and had already lost your sex, long before they ever worshipped you."

The haiku's intense engagement with particular times and places would seem to lend it naturally to the articulation and celebration of local, regional and national identities — although there are those, particularly in America, who are attempting to promote the "globalised haiku" cleansed of "baffling" local idioms and references, and reading in the event like bland translationese. Cobb is against such homogenisation:

I suppose haiku people are among the least nationalistic, probably regarding themselves as a sort of stratum with a similar outlook on life that runs clear through the whole human race. But when they start to look for actual inspiration, that is, at the things and situations in their surroundings that are worth writing about, their local roots will surely — and should surely — assert themselves. I imagine many of us will feel, as I think I do, that we want our roots to suck local soil, but our seeds to blow all over the world.

While commending the inclination of many Welsh, Irish and Scottish poets to address matters of national identity, he feels that in a politically devolved United Kingdom specifically English poetry faces an identity crisis:

The strictly English poets, writing in English-English, have (as in the political world) "lost an empire and not yet found a mission". The geographical, national and cultural references of "English" have been called into question. The need for us writers who are "English" in every sense of the word, to deliver some kind of "Englishness" in our haiku, may therefore be irresistible. A significant feature of this will be the use of vernacular English, not compromising this for the sake of universal intelligibility. One's prime duty is to make sense to one's own community, and to stir it up a bit, and the local images that do this may fall completely flat in the wider domain. Some of us never solve the problem of making sense to our own selves, and surely that is where we all have to begin. It's from the personal and the local that the global may aggregate. Globality may be worth celebrating; personality and diversity certainly are. Identity dies hard — I say, thank goodness! — and communities are distressed if they are dis-embedded from their cultures, which are apt to be defined territorially.

Allegedly Welsh "New Gen" and "Next Gen" pretenders might take note. One feature likely to distinguish English haiku from those of other countries is the nature of their humour. English whimsy does not always travel well — particularly to this corner of Wales: I find pretty excruciating most of the clerihews in Cobb's *The Dead Poets' Cabaret* (Iron Press, 2003), and there are one or two comparable drolleries to be found among the haiku. But the best of his work is richly humorous in a wide variety of ways, from his resourceful playfulness with language:

the breeze this May —
going back time and again
for a free balloon

to kindly parody:

lost in the country —
the roadmender points the way
with his mobile phone

(which refers back in the tradition — as haiku often do — to a famous poem by Issa (1762-1826) — the turnip-puller/points the way/with a turnip), to a McGillian, if not Chaucerian, sauciness:

copper-bottomed
ladies in Bermudas
being camel-humped

to the Rabelaisian:

barbecue —
hairs on the cook's belly
sprinkled with salt

to the cutting irony of two of his best-known senryu (senryu are haiku that tend towards social observation):

rain —
the boat in my neighbour's yard
gets wet at last

breakfast in silence —
both halves of the grapefruit
unsweetened

to the wistful acceptance of transience:

after the snowman
melts into the lawn —
picking up his smile

The very accuracy of Cobb's observations and his intimate familiarity with the world of nature brook no compromise with the globalising approximators and the purveyors of nature-rambling twee. A "cornfield", he knows, is not the same thing to an Essex villager as it is to a maize-growing farmer from Iowa, and he insists on maintaining such distinctions. A distinction he does not entertain, however, is that between humankind and the rest of nature. In the manner of Issa addressing a snail, Cobb will talk directly to a magpie, a beetle, a slug, and in many of his finest haiku there is creative tension between the human, or civilisational, and the natural, as in these two examples:

even on my thumb
the crawling ladybirds
continue mating

evening chill —
mosquitoes tap their beaks
on double glass

As Carol Rumens remarks in her foreword to Palm, "There are no taboos in Cobb's work: sex, war, bodily functions and urban squalor coexist with nightingales and moonlight. The haiku form is treated as a fully functioning vehicle for the contemporary sensibility, and not as a walled garden to which connoisseurs only are invited." Although published by reputable small presses such as Snapshot, Hub, Leap (USA) and Peter Mortimer's admirably haiku-friendly Iron Press, David Cobb has had to take responsibility for publishing the bulk of his most significant work himself — through his own Equinox Press. It is high time that a leading English publisher began dismantling the wall that has been erected against the haiku and the haibun, and gave one of England's most original and engaging writers — in any literary genre — the prominence he deserves.

PLANET 173

The Exchange

Planet invited three haiku practitioners — Nigel Jenkins, Ken Jones, and Lynne Rees — to enter into an email exchange on the subject of haiku and haiku related matters. What follows is an edited-down version of the debate which ensued.

Dear Lynne and Ken,

I'll start off by raising a few points that you might like to get your teeth into. I have just written a (short) history of the haiku in Wales, as an afterword for my forthcoming haiku collection *O for a gun*. In it, I suggest that there has been an improvement in the "acceptability" of haiku and haibun in the "mainstream" magazines, bu we still have a long way to go before the haiku is accorded the same respect and interest as forms, such as the sonnet and terza rima, which have long achieved "indigenised" status. What do you feel are the main reasons for the considerable resistance to the haiku that I'm sure we have all felt in various departments of the literary "mainstream"? And are things getting better? Ken's recent experiences suggest that in Wales, at least, they are not, and that perhaps in this respect my views on the situation are those of what my old pal John Tripp used to call a "twittering optimist". My own feeling is that it's basically a problem of ignorance — that people (including poets, and sophisticated poets at that) simply don't understand how a haiku works and what, in essence, it is. All they seem to "understand" is the wretched syllable count.

With warmest regards,

Nigel

Dear Cymric Haijin,

What I would claim to be authentic haiku are sandwiched between two bastard varieties of pseudo haiku. On the one hand are those entertaining little three liners which don't have any literary pretensions, and so aren't much of a problem. A more serious cause of misunderstanding and dissatisfaction with the genre are poets who otherwise have some standing and authority among their peers. For most of the few haiku found in mainstream journals are pseudo haiku, or, at best, imitations of classical Japanese verses.

Some prominent mainstream poets have indeed made serious attempts at writing haiku. For example, I edited a selection of Tony Conran's haiku and haibun for the British Haiku Society's journal which were highly rated by the members. Yet mainstream poetry critics and reviewers have tended to overlook such work (for example, the ninety haiku in Paul Mundoon's collection *Hay* were largely ignored, even in *Poetry Review*, journal of the Poetry Society of which Muldoon was president). Could those concerned tell us whether their reluctance to comment is due to ignorance and lack of confidence, or just heedless dismissal of the genre?

Hwyl fawr — Ken

Hello Nigel and Ken,

Nigel, you spoke about a problem of ignorance, that even sophisticated poets simply don't understand how a haiku works and what, in essence, it is. Is the problem more that no one, not even haiku poets, can agree what a haiku is? It seems to be a formless form, with no agreement on line count or metre. As a poet writing free verse, and the occasional formal poem, until a year ago, I always worked with the idea that form arose organically from subject matter, that form reinforced and supported the theme and dominant emotional tone. That's something I've carried over into writing haiku: considering line count, line length, line break or enjambment, presence or absence of punctuation with each one I write. Because of the brevity of the form, I'm aware of using a much lighter touch than in longer poems, so the elements of craft don't overpower what I want to say, but it's still the case that the what and how are of primary importance for me.

The majority of the haiku I write don't adhere to the wretched syllable count of 5/7/5, but if there is no form, what is it exactly that differentiates a haiku from any other three line poem? Once again there seems to be no consensus and I come across haiku that are subjective, objective, concrete, metaphorical, suggest a single moment, suggest a period of time.

Looking forward to hearing from you

Best wishes,

Lynne

Dear Ken and Lynne,

Simplicity, clarity, resonance are what I hope to attain in the making of a haiku. The first two qualities are not usually too difficult to achieve, but without resonance — that certain extra something which is far more difficult to define — one's "little word machine" will fail to do more than merely describe, falling short of that transcendent extra step achieved by a fully charged haiku. The result is likely to be the "so what?" haiku, which may be consigned briskly to the "who needs it?" pile. The "free-form" haiku, which seems now to be that preferred by most contemporary English-language haiku poets, may appear, to quote Lynne, "to be a formless form", especially for those who are convinced that the essence of the haiku is a 5-7-5 syllable count. There are, of course, some forms of poetry — such as the limerick or the englyn — so intimately identified with established patterns of rhyme, metre and/or syllable count that to make irresponsibly free with them is effectively to destroy them or to turn them into something quite other: the limerick that doesn't scan properly is about as much use as a fairly accurate knife-thrower.

If all that most "mainstream" poets "know" of the haiku is that it calls for a 5-7-5 syllable count, it's small wonder that masters of intricate forms such as cynghanedd are wont to dismiss the haiku as being too facile to be worthy of their attention — particularly if even the 5-7-5 "rule" has been abandoned by most contemporary English-language haikuists: all that's left, it must appear, is a smudge of directionless verbiage.

I think we may be closer to a broad definitional consensus on the nature of the haiku in this corner of Europe than Lynne allows, thanks partly to the debate stimulated, since 1990, by the British Haiku Society (although the haiku's Welsh specificities remain under-explored). The following are features of the haiku that I consider among its essential characteristics: an innate humility and therefore an instinct to refuse closure, combined with a disinclination to pass comment; a fruitful interplay between the natural and the civilisational; a quality of profound attention, often to minutiae, and a sharpness of observation mediated by down-to-earth, unembellished language; brevity, concision, simplicity, presence, sensory directness and present-tense immediacy; a plain-speaking lack of literary adornment, and the almost complete absence, therefore, of simile; the obliquity of its undemonstrative metaphors; a downplaying of writerly skills (not to mention ego) and its foregrounding of the object and the moment of its attention. I also value Tony Conran's illuminating identification of the three classical haiku attributes: loneliness, tenderness, slenderness.

All the best,

Nigel

Dear Lynne and Nigel,

I am dumbfounded by Lynne's claim that "there seems to be no consensus... about what it is that differentiates a haiku from any other three line poem." An Anglo-American consensus has been developed over the last twenty-five years, and is reflected in hundreds of publications worldwide. Controversy in fact centres on how far we may now venture from "The Consensus" without undermining the potential of the genre which the consensus was designed to enhance. However, I share what I understand to be Nigel's view that too few haiku reach beyond the imagistic — as tiny coiled springs which can release a subtle, fleeting, liberating release from the existential ache of wanting life to be otherwise.

Pushing my reflection
this wheelbarrow
full of rain

To reinforce Nigel's summary of "The Consensus", here are some guidelines with which I open my workshops: Don't search after haiku. Instead, cultivate alertness so you are inspired by authentic experience when it arises. The clarity of such a "haiku moment" should be infused with a warmth of feeling, a shared humanity, as with Osai Ozaki:

Tongs
a mismatched pair
one whole winter

Just relax and keep it simple, without any straining after effect. Avoid cliché, cleverness and wordiness. Thus, Bashôĝ:

Water jar cracks —
I lie awake
this icy night

Many of the best haiku present unexpected and contrasting images. These can arouse profound and subtle emotions and can convey layers of meaning — Nigel's resonance. Often the first line sets the scene, within which the second line makes an observation. The third line then presents an image contrasting with the second line, throwing our normal expectations out of gear, as it were, and opening up a wider perspective which may be both allusive and elusive. There is a mysterious spark of a wider truth here, which is left to the reader's awareness (an "open metaphor"). As for example in Cicely Hill's

Pausing to watch
breeze over the hayfields
forgotten names

The haibun, combining prose in the haiku tradition into which individual haiku are inserted, has no similar" consensus"; I agree with Lynne about the need for haibun of literary quality, well crafted with feeling, imagination, imagery, and an evolved theme (which gives some of them a kinship with a [very] short story).

The haibun is particularly interesting for our present discussion because arguably it can have a stronger cultural identity than haiku. There are undeniably Welsh haibun in English! Being more concrete than English it seems to me that Welsh is the more apt and ready language for haiku. There is a scatter of haiku poets who write in Welsh, but none ever apppears in the mainstream haiku journals (which are all very hospitable to bilingual submissions, particularly Irish and Scots Gaelic).

The Eisteddfod Genedlaethol of 2001 is the only one I know to have had a *Casgliad o Haicw*. The adjudicator was Aled Rhys Wiliam whose criteria clearly mirrored the consensus of the Anglo-American haiku community to which I referred earlier. There were only twelve entrants. Half were judged NOT to have submitted genuine haiku, because their writing was "vers libre" , "informal verses obscure in meaning", "without haiku form except for the three lines and syllable count", "lapsing into cynghanedd", or "only scarce references to nature", or tending to preaching.

The winning haicw by Eirwen George were highly praised in terms of their nature references infused with human feeling, their "taste of Gododdin ", their "split meaning" (presumably the radical swerve commonly between lines 2 and 3), and their crafted quality in terms of the Japanese classical tradition. Here are three of her haiku, translated by Noragh Jones, and reproduced with grateful acknowledgement.

Diferion o haul	drops of sunlight
Yn gloywi glas y tonnau	brightening the grey waves
Ar Ddydd Ffwl Ebrill	on April Fool's Day
Wêc ar y tonnau	a wake on the waves

| *Yn lledu, yn toddi'n ddim* | widening, dissolving to nothing |
| *Fel ein taith ninnau* | like our own journey |

Gwynt yn y dderwen	wind in the oak tree
A'i grafanc am ddeilen grin	clawing a withered leaf
Egni marwolaeth	the energy of death

I understand that an anthology to be published by Gwasg Carreg Gwalch will be predominantly English language and selected because of their Welsh subject matter alone. The difficulty of selecting them by any other distinctively Welsh criterion will be appreciated. For my part I believe that it is still the job of the bard to celebrate the national landscape, history, legends and heroes, and I have done so with relish in my three successive volumes of haibun and haiku (including two well researched victories of Owain Glyndŵr).

This may be gratifying politically, of course, but doesn't take us very far from a literary point of view. I do believe, however, that in much Welsh writing in English it is possible to discern a distinctive Welsh sensibility. Doubtless this has been discussed at length elsewhere, and probably isn't worth pursuing much here: we write what we write, and can do no other. In my collection, *The Parsley Bed*, the haibun set in a Welsh hairdressing salon, or that in praise of Dovey Junction, are surely Welsh in much more than subject, but that's just how I write. However, I am still curious about such Welshness.

Pob hwyl — Ken

Dear Ken and Lynne,

By no means all of the (by now) couple of dozen serious (as opposed to occasional) haiku writers working in Wales would see themselves as operating in a Welsh literary context, and there are doubtless some who choose to remain in ignorance of that context (odd and culturally irresponsible as such detachment has always seemed to me). The haiku's intense engagement with particular times and places would seem to lend it naturally to the articulation and celebration of local, regional and national identities — although there are those, particularly in America, who are attempting to promote the "globalised haiku" cleansed of "baffling" local idioms and references. While I am with the English haiku poet David Cobb (and others) in resisting such bland homogenisation, I would hope to avoid, in my own haiku, any striving after deliberate Welsh effect. I desire, above all, to make affecting haiku. If some Welshness in such haiku is also discernible — then fine, that's a bonus; but I don't want to compromise the integrity of my haiku with heavy-handed flag waving. It will be interesting to see what is Welsh about the haiku that Arwyn Evans has gathered together for the Gwasg Carreg Gwalch anthology.

Cofion cynnes,
Nigel

Dear Nigel and Ken,

The closest I can come to identifying a "Welsh sensibility" for myself is in the rhythm of how I write. I write for my own spoken voice (which, through no effort at all, has retained its accent despite 29 years away from Wales), my inflection and intonation, and I generally dislike anyone else reading my poetry aloud. I have had some poems criticised for being unrhythmical on the page, but that criticism has been withdrawn when I've read them aloud.

I rarely write explicitly about Wales, though my imagery often has its roots there, particularly when it comes to the sea,

145

mountains, and working-class communities, though I don't wish to impose their Welshness on any reader, and would prefer that they translate those images to illuminate and reinforce their own experiences and emotional connections to their own lives.

Then there's colloquial expression and pronunciation. In my family, we say "knock" the light off for "switch" the light off... though I'm yet to find any other Welsh person who says that too! And there's daps, poop, twty down, tumps, a joking fire (as opposed to a real one). When I'm teaching syllabic verse at the University of Kent I have to remind myself, for the purpose of the exercise, that "fire" has one syllable. Or, when I'm reading a poem aloud to the class, to say "here" with an aspirated h, not a y, because it's just too distracting to drop in that peculiarity. Is this Welshness? Or just me-ness?

I don't think that a poet's primary role has to be the celebration of the national landscape, history, culture; doesn't that suggest that a poet who doesn't write in celebration of these things, isn't as worthy? What about the poet who explores the emotional landscape; territory that crosses boundaries of race and origin, and celebrates the universal human experience? A haibun can accommodate narrative tension, character development, exposition... the things necessary for a good story based on historical or contemporary events, but there certainly isn't room to do that in the haiku, which I've begun to think of as the shortest lyric form available to us. The idea too that the haiku creates "some warmth in feeling, a shared humanity" is underpinned by its structure in often bringing together disparate things to create a sense of unity. I find that very exciting — a form that has, at its core, the idea of unity.

Best Wishes,

Lynne

Dear Lynne and Nigel,

It appears that we each have had three innings, and the deadline suggests it's indeed time to wrap up! In parenthesis, I'd just like to observe that I didn't claim that it was the job of the Welsh poet to celebrate the nation, but of the "BARD"! Both Nigel and I have a habit of going into bardic mode sometimes.

Pob hwyl — Ken

PLANET 183

References: Lee Gurga, *Haiku: A Poet's Guide* (Modern Haiku Press, 2003); William J. Higginson, *The Haiku Handbook* (Kodansha International, 1989); Jane Reichhold, *Writing and Enjoying Haiku: A Hands-on Guide* (Kodansha International, 2002)
Websites: www.redthreadhaiku.org
www.contemporaryhaibunonline.com

Poetry at the Valley Folk Club, Pontardawe

Nigel Jenkins

It may have been my mixing it with folk musicians — with a tour of Gower pubs that I organised in 1977, featuring the Swansea folk group Cromlech and a rotating roster of local poets — that led to my being invited by the Valley Folk Club to provide them with the odd (sometimes very odd) poet. Quite a few folk fans came to those gratifyingly well attended monthly performances, and I remember reading at another event that summer — a twmpath, of sorts, in a barn at Knelston — with Swansea Jack and others, and chatting to Mick Tems, Mike James, Pete Davies and Ruth Exhall about poetry and folk cross-connections, and the potential for making more of them.

I can't remember exactly when the club's organisers first invited me to fix them up with a poet or two, but it was probably some time after I had become a regular member of the audience during the later 1970s. Nor can I remember for sure all the poets I brought along, and the order in which, over the years, they appeared there. But certain poets and certain evenings still spring vibrantly to mind, and in response to a request from Gwyn Jones for my recollections,[1] I summon here what I can from the fogs of memory — although imposing any reliable chronology on them is, I'm afraid, beyond me.

The club was always wonderfully receptive of poetry — which is not surprising, really, when you consider the rapt attention with which its audiences have always listened to the words of songs being sung to them. There is poetry — sometimes hair-raisingly powerful poetry — in folk songs, and the club's audiences are finely attuned to it. Not infrequently on club nights a singer or a member of the audience would recite a favourite poem in among the songs, and there would be original poetry from local poets such as Brian Smith, who has long had a talent to entertain, and move, with his light (and not-so-light) verse.

I wanted to invite poets who could take the stage and address an audience, not poets — no matter how affecting their poetry — who'd cower behind their pages and mumble into their beards. A fitting early choice, therefore, was Swansea-born Harri Webb, famous throughout Wales for his impassioned, satirical, sometimes angry, sometimes lyrical readings and performances with groups such as Pryderi and His Pigs and for appearances on television shows such as *Poems and Pints*. Harri was a forceful performer who could work the silences and hold with a word fifty or sixty people, many of whom might never have attended a poetry reading. He exulted in putting the boot in where necessary, scandalising the genteel, and upsetting political opponents; he relished flying in the face of that 'ghastly good taste' which, he said, was 'one of the pervading weaknesses of the Anglo-Welsh generally'.

As a republican, socialist and nationalist, Harri had much in common with another early guest to the club, the Cardiff poet John Tripp. They often read their poetry from the same platforms. But they differed in at least one important respect. Where Harri, for all his frolicsome sociability, remained an intensely private person, temperamentally disinclined to make art out of the griefs and foibles of selfhood, Tripp was unashamedly an individualist who built his poetry around the goings-on and gettings-up-to — laughter, tears, farts 'n' all — of a persona more or less identifiable with the poet himself. Once he came over to Pontardawe at festival time, to read in the regular poetry fringe event that was held in the Victoria. It was followed (as usual with John) by a booze-up on the *maes* of festive proportions — and then, long after nightfall, he mysteriously disappeared, and was not seen again until the following morning: he'd slept the night on a stretcher in the St John's Ambulance tent.

Both poets, in their different ways, held the club audience spellbound. No doubt they did much to convince the unpersuaded that the 'intrusion' of poets into a folk milieu was not, after all, such a questionable thing, and to lay a worthwhile foundation for poets to come. Sometimes they'd be poets from the Swansea area, such as J.C. Evans, Penny Windsor and Malcolm Parr, with his wry social commentaries and his brilliant Lorca translations (later described by Allen Ginsberg as the best he'd ever encountered). The Hafod-born painter Jack Jones took to the stage one night, and, fuelled with red wine and surely a pill or two, went on, and on, and on, oblivious to the fact that he had vastly exceeded his allotted ten minutes; as the audience shuffled, checked their watches and yawned, Jack droned on, getting slower and slower, until he eventually fell sound asleep, standing up at the lectern, like an old carthorse dozing on all fours in the corner of a field. A livelier routine was provided by Jan Smith, the doggerelizing landlady from a pub in Caegarw, who liked dolling herself up as a witch to deliver her mock-macabre ditties.

Sometimes we'd look further afield, and bring in a poet with a major international reputation such as Adrian Mitchell who, since he first became famous around the time of the Albert Hall readings of 1968 ('Tell me lies about Vietnam …'), has maintained a reputation as one of the most compelling poetry performers in these islands. Like Webb and Tripp (both now, alas, no longer with us), Adrian is able skilfully to vary the pace and tone of a reading, alternating the high seriousness of an angry celebration of the Chilean folk-singer Victor Jara, murdered by the fascist junta in 1973, with, say, the absurd knockabout of a poem such as 'Ten ways to avoid lending your wheelbarrow to anyone' (i.e. 'May I borrow your wheelbarrow?' 'Only if I can fuck your wife in it.'). Adrian, who lives in London, asked me to fix him up with a school reading as well as the one at the club — to make the trip worth his while. 'How many kids do you want to read to?' I asked. 'As many as you like,' he said, 'Fill the hall.'

I took him at his word. The event is remembered in a horror poem entitled 'The Olchfa Reading' and beginning 'I had told Nigel Jenkins / the bard of Mumbles, who was my friend, / that I wanted to read to a large audience ...' (note that 'was'). The poem goes on to describe his encounter 'in a hall the size of / a Jumbo Jet hanger' with a crowd 'as multitudinous / as the armies of Genghis Khan / but they were larger and hairier / and less interested in poetry'. Well, at least Adrian got a poem out of it — one of his comic masterpieces, in fact. A packed and appreciative house at the Dynevor Arms that night more than made up for his Olchfa nightmare.

Another memorable traveller from afar was the Glaswegian poet Tom Leonard whose political and social satire, couched in pungent Glasgow dialect, is as sharp as the sharpest of diamonds, and not for the politically faint of heart. He read at the club around the time of the United States' imperialist blockade — by warship and mine — of one of the principal ports of Nicaragua. I remember Tom raising a mighty laugh (and one or two ruffled eyebrows) by tiptoeing around on stage, making bomb noises, leaping into the air — and asking the audience who he was. Answer: Jesus Christ walking on the waters of the Bay of Nicaragua.

When the club moved to the Ivy Bush, the occasional poetry spots continued — but not for many years longer, thanks to the unforgettable appearance there of Ifor 'Chainsaw' Thomas. Ifor, well-established in Cardiff and beyond as an iconoclastic performance poet without parallel in the English-shouting world, came equipped for his reading with a pub-style chair, an armful of fat literary tomes (which he said represented the collected works of venerable poets such as Shakespeare, Milton and Wordsworth), a roll of cling-film, a rather bewitching young Gothette of a poet (but that's another story) — and a chainsaw. He climaxed his reading — executed, as ever, without the safety net of a written text — by hollering forth his poem, about seeing off the fusty bardic elders, while piling up the tomes on the chair and securing them there with lashings of cling-film. Then he turned to the chainsaw, revved it roaringly, and proceeded to saw through the piled tomes and the chair, spouting forth inaudibly as the chainsaw ripped through *King Lear, Paradise Lost* and *The Lyrical Ballads*. At this point the landlord walked in and was furious to see Ifor sawing through what he assumed to be one of his pub's chairs. 'If this is poetry,' he exploded, 'there'll be no more of it in any pub of mine. Beer and chainsaws do not mix.' (An observation, indeed, not entirely devoid of a modicum of truth.)

And thus, abruptly, poetry's intermittent — but I hope rewarding — run at the Valley Folk Club came to an end. During those years, and for a year or two afterwards — up until about 1986, when changing nappies took over from organising poetry readings — I was also charged with running poetry readings during the festival.

These fringe events, held usually in a back room at the Vic around lunchtime on the Saturday and the Sunday, were distinctly low-key affairs, with usually no more than about a dozen — mostly poets (and a domineering snooker table) — in attendance, although the poetry was often of the highest calibre, issuing from the pens of some of Wales's finest poets. Both Webb and Tripp were guests at the Vic, and Tony Conran, assisted by his wife Lesley, read there most years, Tony being perhaps the most committed and best informed folk aficionado among the poets of Wales. Other Vic regulars at festival time included Chris O'Neil, Eddie Lunt, Terry Hetherington — and anyone, indeed, who felt like contributing a poem. These modest, under-promoted gatherings in the Vic were stimulating and congenial, but I regret not being able to persuade the festival organisers to put poetry on the main stage — in the person, say, of Adrian Mitchell, Hamish Henderson or Ifor Thomas (with or without chainsaw). Not all poets would be up to a main-stage slot, but some are consummate performers who would be capable of enthralling a Pontardawe audience.

I don't know whether all the poets I have inflicted on the club over the years have been good for Pontardawe, but Pontardawe has been generously hospitable towards a wide range of poets, and I thank the organisers, Gwyn Jones above all, for their encouragement of poetry at the Valley Folk Club. It would be good to see that chainsaw-disrupted tradition revived.

1. For the club's fortieth anniversary celebrations in September 2008.

The Harri Webb Prize, 2004

Although there was no outright winner in the competition for a poem to commemorate Owain Glyndŵr, on the occasion of the 600th anniversary of his historic parliament at Machynlleth, there were two poems deemed worthy of sharing the prize — which is awarded periodically, usually for a collection of poems, to a poet writing in the genres or spirit, or on the kind of subjects that exercised the republican, socialist and nationalist energies of Harri Webb (1920-94). The competition judges, Nigel Jenkins, Sally Roberts Jones and Meic Stephens (trustees of the Harri Webb Prize), chose as joint winners Herbert Williams's "Owain Glyndŵr" and Tom Cheesman's "Owain Glyndŵr Explained to an Algerian Asylum Seeker" — that asylum seeker being the fine Swansea-based poet Soleïman Adel Guémar; they receive £150 each. Mandy Pannett's "Open Letter to Owen Glendower" was awarded £50 as runner-up.

The competition attracted about thirty poems from twenty-five individual contenders. That there were relatively few entries (despite there being no entry fee), and that most of the offerings were unimpressive was disappointing — but hardly surprising. Since the late 1970s, there has been very little encouragement for forthrightly political poetry; indeed, the critical climate — conditioned by the Audenesque view that "poetry makes nothing happen", which is hardly in accord with Welsh experience — has been generally disdainful of the political and historical subject matter that inspired much of the best (and some of the worst) poetry of the generation of English-language poets that came to prominence in the 1960s. The difficulties of writing political poetry, particularly in celebration of a national hero, should not be underestimated, and the potential pitfalls are many: earnest "we will rise again" triumphalism, musty heraldic rhetoric, pseudo-medieval romanticism, galumphing doggerel, tensionless and simplistic regurgitations of the story, prosy sloganeering unacquainted with the sophisticated potential of language — to name but the most obvious.

About half a dozen efforts strove to avoid such pitfalls, although it was generally the case that in sidestepping the temptations of swashbuckling doggerel they merely lumbered themselves with the flat rhythms of chopped prose. As Sally Roberts Jones noted, it was often the technique that let the writer down: "Strict verse needs flexible rhythms, but not jagged ones, and free verse needs the poet's own rhythm or it stays simply prose. It's surprising how many would-be poets lack an ear for rhythm — it's as if a singer were tonedeaf."

Easily the most imaginative — if wildly anachronistic — treatment of the subject was Tom Cheesman's, which used the mysterious "disappearance" of Glyndŵr at the end of the Revolt to invent a startling later career for him: captured at sea by Barbary corsairs and sold into slavery in Algeria, where he passed into legend as Wan Ben-el-Qumri or Awen Ath-Qlad-Yur.

Herbert Williams, identifying in Glyndŵr a perennial ambiguity, samples several ways in which he has been portrayed, from the romantic "hero of a fleeting hour", to Shakespeare's "Welsh wizard" and the "terrorist" of the Raffa Club, where only Bomber Harris is sanctioned to kill. Williams concludes inconclusively, in "a mess of intimations", but he is in no doubt about the formative influence on modern Wales of Glyndŵr's revolt: "All that's happened since/ followed from that". Because *Planet*, anticipating an outright winner, had bargained on only one poem, lack of space precludes publication of the two (longish) prize-winning entries. They can be read, however, on the *Planet* website in the Current Issue section: www.planet magazine. org.uk

Nigel Jenkins: Foreword to
Burning the Candle by Christine Evans

In a country which has produced a surprisingly large number of long poems in the English language — from, say, Vernon Watkins's *Ballad of the Mari Lwyd* and Idris Davies's *The Angry Summer* in the earlier twentieth century to Chris Torrance's *The Diary of Palug's Cat*, Gillian Clarke's *Letter from a Far Country* and John Barnie's *Ice* in more recent times — few are more accomplished in the genre than Christine Evans. *Burning the Candle* — 1160 lines of poetry composed, remarkably, in only four weeks (as were, at the same time, the fourteen impressive 'spin-off' poems) — confirms her reputation as one of the most compelling and distinctive poets of contemporary Wales.

Born in Yorkshire in 1943, she came to her father' birthplace, Pwllheli, in 1967 to teach English (from which she took early retirement in 1997). She married into a family which had been farming on the island of Enlli (Bardsey) since 1770. The farming — in which, as her poetry shows, she also became actively involved — has by now given way to fishing, boat-building and ferrying tourists, but the island still plays a central role in the family's life. She, her husband Ernest and their son Col continue, after wintering on the mainland (at Aberdaron), to spend the summer months on Enlli. The perceptive and warmly sympathetic poetry she has written about her adoptive community, from her 1983 debut onwards, testifies to the commitment and sensitivity with which she has grafted herself onto the culture.

The long poem, which should be distinguished from the poem sequence, tends to be viewed as something of an oddity — voracious of time and energy to write, and then extremely difficult to find

156

outlets for. The twenty to fifty-line lyric poem favoured by the literary journals may be regarded today as the norm, but most of the great poetry of ancient and oral cultures has been long, promulgating an integrated vision of life and dealing with spiritual and cosmological matters of the profoundest public importance. Many long poems, such as Homer's Odyssey (which Christine Evans was re-reading as she wrote this poem), are narrative epics; others, particularly those of modernist and postmodernist times, are epics of the mind, and it is to this category that *Burning the Candle* belongs. It has fragmented narrative elements, certainly, but it achieves its structural cohesion through procedures that are analogous to those of the symphony. It is an intimate meditation — about light, yes, but also about life, death, science, creativity, hope, despair, continuity, and much else. Acknowledging unflinchingly 'the dark areas' and drawing no solace from religion, this literally wonder-ful poem is nevertheless a celebration of life. 'I am wondering ...' she says, in both senses of a term that makes a direct, involving appeal to 'the reader / I have to believe in / somewhere, letting it happen.' The questing, welcoming personality of the poet persuades us (as does Chaucer's in *The Canterbury Tales*) to spend time in her company on the poem's journey — all long poems, of course, being something of a pilgrimage.

Any reader of *Burning the Candle* will surely find the accompanying log a fascinating insight into both the creative process and the nature of the long poem. There are, by now, innumerable accounts by poets of how they have crafted their lyric poems, but I can think of no reflection on the making of a long poem which is as open, honest, detailed and tense with creative drama as this absorbing 'thinking aloud' journal. With the additional '7 Steps towards the Long Poem', this book is likely to prove a must for creative writing booklists throughout the land.

GOMER PRESS MARCH 2006

'O what can you give me?'

Nigel Jenkins on Idris Davies

'Why read Idris Davies today?' seemed to be the burden of it when the editor invited me to write an article to mark the centenary of the poet's birth.

It can hardly be claimed that in his own time Idris Davies (1905-53) was a fashionable poet, nor at any time since can he be said to have been in vogue among the arbiters of literary taste. Few readers of poetry, coming new to Idris Davies and leafing through his pages for the first time, would be likely to find themselves much persuaded by the plentiful 'o'er's and 'whate'er's, the monotonous metres, predictable rhymes and rhyme-serving inversions, the apocalyptic socialist victories. Many of his poems resort to literary devices that were outmoded well before the twentieth century, let alone the twenty-first. But to dismiss him as unambitiously old-fashioned or to patronise him as a minor although interesting 'regional' writer, not bad for a scion of the working class, is to misconstrue him entirely. For Idris Davies eventually succeeded — albeit, sadly, after his death — in achieving the not inconsiderable ambition of writing poetry that would be both popular and significant among his not-especially-literary countrymen and women — to such an extent that his books, over the years, have sold in their thousands rather than in the couple of hundred that is the fate of most poetry collections.

Although he is nowhere near being the kind of household name in Wales that 'national poets' such as Lorca and Neruda are in their countries, Idris Davies matters to relatively large numbers of his compatriots in ways that most poets of the latest fleeting moment do not, and he is preferred by many to poets with much grander reputations, such as Dylan Thomas and R.S. Thomas. He has also

158

achieved popularity among millions in the wider world, thanks to Pete Seeger's setting of *Gwalia Deserta* XV ('The Bells of Rhymney'), which was a massive hit for The Byrds in the mid 1960s and which — with Rhymney all too often mispronounced to rhyme with 'chimney'— has been recorded by scores of performers since, among them Emmylou Harris, the McGarrigle sisters and Bob Dylan. And he has been influential: without his shade's numinous presence in the hills around Merthyr, it is possible that this magazine would not have been founded, and it is probable that without his 'permission' some of the liveliest and most engaging writers of *Poetry Wales*'s early years would not have come to fruition. Harri Webb, John Tripp (Rhymney-born, like Idris Davies) and others — the Idrisiaid (sons of Idris), as Tony Conran has called them[1] — took up where Idris Davies left off, as socially engaged poets in the Welsh tradition, promoting a socialist, republican and nationalist politics, using many of Davies's populist devices (especially in Webb's case), and falling, sometimes, into many of his rhetorical, sentimental and generalising bad habits. The Idrisiaid were top swashbuckling dogs for a while, but they fell somewhat out of official favour during the 1970s; this magazine's rejection of one of the decade's finest poems, Harri Webb's 'That Summer', was a chilly portent of a change in the wind's general direction. Although, by the mid 1980s, incapacity (Webb) and death (Tripp) — not to mention 'the dream and swift disaster' of the 1979 Devolution referendum — had silenced the most voluble voices of the tribe, the Idrisiaid and their fellow travellers were by no means vanquished. Herbert Williams and the underrated Alun Rees, who had been in at the beginning of Meic Stephens's revolution, continue to keep the faith, and a number of younger poets, among them Mike Jenkins, Dave Hughes and Grahame Davies (the last named in both Welsh and English), emerged from the pluralist bush with a strong mark of Idris upon them. In the meantime, academe has caught up, and Idris Davies has long been studied in university English and

Welsh-studies departments. So why, then, does this dead red poet still cause a stir?

With fewer than 400 miners working underground (and about 360 working in open-cast mines), the south Wales coalfield is today, basically, a worked-out mining camp. That, however, it remains home to half the inhabitants of Wales is the central challenge facing the nation as a whole, and consciousness of its remarkable history is fundamental to the condition of being Welsh. Although the poetry of Idris Davies deserves to be valued as a unique document in the nurturing of that consciousness — particularly consciousness of the socially devastating Depression of the 1930s[2] — it is of very much more than historical significance, for his world is still, in essence, all too recognisably ours. The pit-head wheels and tips may have disappeared from the landscape, but 'the callous economics of a world / Whose god is Mammon' remain as damaging and threatening as ever. Still with us, often in more acute forms than in Idris Davies's day, and making a mockery of his desire that there be 'as much beauty as possible in our everyday lives', are wage slavery (much of the worst of it exported by now to the world's poorest countries), obscene discrepancies in wealth, environmental devastation, rampant imperialism (American more than British these days), an idiotic and venal press, fetishistic consumerism, and fundamentalist, intolerant religions. Such are Idris Davies's far from old-fashioned concerns, and he is as apprehensive as any modern eco-poet that

Already we smell the carcass of civilisation,
A huge grey carcass stretched out across the ruins
And rotting in the rain.

('The Carcass')

He sometimes comes close to relishing such despair — a despair that carries considerably more weight than the solution proposed in the theatrical trumpetry of 'The Socialist Victory'. Less woozy with unconvincing rhetoric is the belief in the power of action based on rational analysis that finds expression in 'Come Unto These Yellow Sands' (unpublished in his lifetime):

O when you lie upon the sands
And gaze far out to sea,
Remember you can train those hands
To alter history!

— although it is vain to look for a consistent political 'line' in his poetry. Aestheticism, a powerful attraction throughout Idris Davies's writing life, sometimes tipped the balance against the social and political impulse, particularly in later life when, increasingly, he 'hated the vulgar and the meretricious / Be their colour red or Tory blue' and sought a somewhat solipsist refuge in singing of 'the beauty lost and the beauty yet to be'. Exceptionally well read and a man of rich and complex intellect, he was capable — like Harri Webb later — of writing sophisticated and demanding poetry that even experienced readers find challenging (some of his Dylanesque forays into surrealism are beyond me). But, also like Harri Webb, he consciously imposed limitations on the formal development of his poetry, resorting unashamedly to accessible and traditional modes in most of the work by which he is best remembered, pre-eminently the two masterpieces *Gwalia Deserta* (1938) and *The Angry Summer* (1943). He was quite clear about what he was doing:

'I am a socialist,' he wrote in his diary. 'That is why I want as much beauty as possible in our everyday lives, and so am an enemy of pseudo-poetry and pseudo-art of all kinds. Too many "poets of the Left", as they call themselves, are badly in need of instruction as to the difference between poetry and propaganda. … These people

should read Blake on Imagination till they show signs of understanding him. Then the air would be clear again, and the land be, if not full of, fit for song.[3]

Unlike many poets self-consciously of the 1930s Left — the middle-class intellectuals of the 'Macspaunday' school, with their somewhat willed and theoretical Marxism that soon enough fizzled out into liberalism, Christianity and despair — Idris Davies was 'of the line', born among the people and into the class to whom and for whom, primarily, he wanted to speak; his revolt against capitalism came from direct experience of some of its worst consequences. The modernism of Joyce, Lorca, Dylan Thomas, Eliot and others was important to him as both reader and writer, but he was all too conscious of 'Ianto bach Rees who had never heard of T.S. Eliot'; he was convinced that a poetry about the southern coalfield using modernist strategies would succeed only in erecting impenetrable barriers between himself and his intended audience. The desire to speak 'appropriate language' to his people drew from Geoffrey Grigson, in a review of *Gwalia Deserta* in New Verse, 31/32 (1938), the taunt that the book was the product of 'a simple and superficial mind' — to which Idris Davies replied:

… I certainly was not surprised to see it called 'simple'. I wish it were simpler than it is, for even now it is too 'difficult' for some folk in South Wales — the folk whom I have tried to write about, the folk who have never heard of NEW VERSE and literary cliques.

Without any hesitation, I admit that Gwalia Deserta is simple, but I think you do me an injustice when you say it is superficial. I have written about coal-miners, employed and unemployed, in as realistic a way as I possibly could. I did not try to be pretty-pretty about them. I tried to give an objective account of the whole show. When

I tell you that I worked for 7 years in the coal-face, I think you will
agree that I had some practical knowledge of my subject.
It would have been very easy to make Gwalia Deserta *obscure …*
I did what I could do, openly and honestly, and I let the book take
any chance it had.[4]

In rejecting a modernist approach, he opted instead for what it is possible to recognise today as postmodern techniques. Daniel Williams, in a fascinating comparison of Idris Davies with the black American poet Langston Hughes (1902-67),[5] identifies remarkable parallels in their attitudes to their intended readership and their perceived roles as poets, and in poetic strategies that were rooted in the popular culture of their time and respective places. He points to corresponding emphases, in a passage from Langston Hughes's essay 'The Negro Artist and the Racial Mountain' (1926), on personal experience and objective honesty:

But then there are the low-down folks, the so-called common
element, and they are the majority — may the Lord be praised! The
people who have their nip of gin on Saturday nights and are not too
important to themselves or the community, or too well fed, or too
learned to watch the lazy world go round … Their joy runs, bang!
into ecstasy. Their religion soars to a shout. Work maybe a little
today, rest a little tomorrow. Play awhile. Sing awhile. O, let's dance!
These common people are not afraid of spirituals … and jazz is their
child. They furnish a wealth of colourful, distinctive material for any
artist because they still hold their own individuality in the fact of
American standardizations … Most of my own poems are racial in
theme and treatment, derived from the life I know. In many of them
I try to grasp and hold some of the meanings and rhythms of jazz.
I am as sincere as I know how to be.

Just as Langston Hughes — as capable as Idris Davies of writing in Standard English 'literary' mode — favoured the informality of Black English in order to appeal to the largest possible constituency, so Idris Davies, whose first language was Welsh and who remained a passionate advocate of Welsh, chose to write mainly in English (by then the language of the majority in the eastern valleys) in order to connect with the widest audience. (He was easy with both languages in a way that remained exceptional among writers in either 'camp' until the 1980s, when a new rapprochement began to mature — a further instance of his beneficial example.) Then there's the eagerness with which both poets founded much of their poetry on the rhythms, sounds, structures and references of the music and poetry that was popular in their day: for the American, spirituals, blues, jazz and proverbial sayings; for the Welshman, Nonconformist hymns, biblical texts, music hall and folk songs, jazz, playground chants, the oratory of pulpit and soapbox, and the sentimental and patriotic verse of poets such as John Ceiriog Hughes (1832-87) (not, perhaps, such cosy homespun as you might think: when Allen Ginsberg came to Wales in 1995 there were just two poets the avant-garde Beatmeister was eager to meet — although he was a little too late for one of them: Dic Jones and Ceiriog). They also had in common, as Daniel Williams observes, a romantic *hiraeth* for a far distant, legendary past in which their now humiliated and culturally impoverished peoples were fulfilled and dignified: Africa for one, and for the other a Celtic past when 'the harp and bugle / Stirred the fettered to be free ...'.

A postmodernist reappraisal such as this encourages an appreciation of those fragmentations, inconsistencies, contradictions and conflicting registers that have often been condemned as flaws in the poetry of Idris Davies. As Dafydd Johnston states in his introduction to *The Complete Poems*, 'Postmodernism recognizes the essentially self-referential nature of the literary process, that is the ways in which works of literature derive from and define themselves by reference to other works. Viewed in this light the fragmentation can be seen to be a central and definitive aspect of Idris Davies's work, rather than an unfortunate weakness.'

Another aspect of Idris Davies's appeal that should not be underestimated is his humour, the full scope of which could not be appreciated until the appearance in *The Complete Poems* of his uncollected and previously unpublished work. It has many registers and purposes: the generously affirmative and celebratory underpinning of his social observations ('Tiger Bay'); the affectionate rib-tickling of, say, the versified joke, 'Singing Sospan Fach'; the exuberant wordplay of 'Our Vegetarians'; the wry needling of religious hypocrisy, as in the justly renowned 'Capel Calvin'; and the full-frontal, furious, satirical demolition — often in no more than four lines — of such targets as the mineowner, the City fixer, the turncoat politician, the slum landlord, the lie-mongering press — and, for example, 'The Crooner':

Here comes that squalid, spineless creature
  That smirks and screams and groans,
A fungus spawned one night when Nature
  Ran short of brains and bones.

— who could be some talentless egomaniac from a 'reality' show. Subtle and genteel this ain't, but it does its job and still has its uses over half a century after it was written. The Idrisiaid have always understood the power of humour (see, for instance, the barbed wit of the Taffy poems that Alun Rees published in *Radical Wales*), but there is little encouragement of it in today's magazines, which tend to favour only the kind of world-weary, clever-dick irony that is desperate to avoid any serious commitment to anything.

Idris Davies also goes usefully against the grain in his enthusiasm for voices and masks. Critical orthodoxy has long insisted on the importance of a poet 'finding a voice' and, having got it, supergluing that priceless commodity to his or her bardic being. The example of Idris Davies encourages us to ignore such calls to monovocal bliss and to listen instead to the wayward voice of each new poem — many poems, many voices. This is not simply a question of the multiplicity of particular or representative voices heard in such effective dramatic counterpoint in a poem such as *The Angry Summer*; it is to do with the 'unreliability' or inconsistency of what is assumed to be the poet's 'own' voice — so that, for instance, he seems in some poems to identify himself with the mountain-top 'dreamer', whereas in others he is angrily impatient with the dreamer's failure to confront reality; another instance of very disparate first-person voicings occurs with *Gwalia Deserta* XXIV and XXV, where XXV — 'Who seeks another kingdom / Beyond the common sky?' — draws on hymnal language to comment on the obviously more personal free-verse subject matter of XXIV — 'Because I was sceptical in our Sunday School / And tried to picture Jesus crawling in the local mine …'. Much has been made of *The Angry Summer* as a play for voices, but there are many voices at play in *Gwalia Deserta* too, albeit more covertly, so that, like a Cubist painting, the view is multifaceted, complex and resistant to a single, domineering interpretation of society and events; it is alive with contending possibilities. Any contemporary poet interested in the potential of the long poem or the poem-sequence — forms little attempted these days — could learn much from the example of Idris Davies. My own long(ish) *Circus* (1979) owes almost everything, structurally, to the Idris Davies model, and it would be surprising if Barry MacSweeney's formidable 55-section poem *Black Torch* (1978) did not owe something to Idris Davies (although it is too late now to ask MacSweeney, who died in 2000).

The literary devices that have sometimes seen Idris Davies slighted by the critics were the direct result of his chosen stance as a poet. As a people's remembrancer, who wrote a great deal that is deeply affecting and wonderfully memorable, he was not content to closet himself away in the lonely wardrobes of hermetic incomprehensibility and social irrelevance. Wanting urgently to communicate with his people, he set out, with almost scientific precision, to do so — and there is more, still, that should be done to help him in this. The publication of *The Complete Poems* in 1994 exposed the inadequacy of Gomer's *Collected*, which first appeared in 1972 and which, six printings later, was reissued in 2003 with a splendidly combative introduction by Jim Perrin. There is surely a need, especially with the (expensive and academic) *Complete Poems* out of print, for a *Selected Poems* that weeds out some of the feebler offerings of the *Collected* and makes room for many important poems that have not yet been given a chance to connect with a popular readership, among them 'The Collier Boy', 'Singing Sospan Fach', a host of satirical and comic poems, and the shamefully neglected 36-poem sequence *Gwalia My Song*, which deserves to take its place alongside *Gwalia Deserta* and *The Angry Summer* as among Idris Davies's greatest achievements.

POETRY WALES 40/4 - 2005

1. Tony Conran, '*Poetry Wales* and the Second Flowering' in M. Wynn Thomas (ed.), *Welsh Writing in English* (University of Wales Press, 2003).
2. Gwyn A. Williams wrote in 'Mother Wales, get off me back?' (*Marxism Today*, December 1981): 'In terms of social disruption and identity crisis, the depression plays the same role in Welsh history as the famine in Irish.'
3. Quoted from R George Thomas's introduction to *The Collected Poems of Idris Davies* (Gomer, 1972), p. xvii.
4. *New Verse*, new series, no. 1 (1939).
5. Daniel Williams, 'Y Coch a'r Du: Moderniaeth a Chenedligrwydd yn Harlem a Chymru' in M. Wynn Thomas (ed.), *Gweld Sêr — Cymru a Chanrif America* (Gwasg Prifysgol Cymru, 2001).

Childe Roland
to Welsh Obscurity Came

Nigel Jenkins profiles the concrete poet Childe Roland

There are not many artists of Wales whose work has been exhibited alongside the works of Picasso, Matisse, Duchamp, Magritte, Marinetti, Braque, John Cage and Man Ray. In fact, there is probably only one, although few in Wales have heard of him: the trilingual concrete poet from Llangollen, Childe Roland (whose real name is Peter Noël Meilleur).

Avant-garde adventurers in the visual arts have long been more positively received hereabouts than those who have striven to "make it new" in the literary field. There has been room for only one (part-time) concrete poet in Wales, Peter Finch, whose acceptability has been predicated partly on the reassuringly "mainstream" inclination of his other endeavours. For thirty years, the Québecois from Llangollen, whose remarkable verbal and material creations are unlike anything seen or heard in this (or any other) country, has ploughed a solitary furrow, routinely disdained and rebuffed by journals, publishers, venues and the Arts Council, and greeted with bafflement and derision by those who have been impatient to dismiss him before they have properly examined what he's about. That he has been published by no one but himself (he describes himself, accordingly, as "unpublished") arouses in him a mixture of anger, disappointment — and modest pride, for there's a purist determination about him which, aesthetically, will give no moderating quarter. "It is sad that the Arts Council and the literary magazines of Wales pretend I do not exist," he wrote to me in 2005. "I guess they are waiting for the Parkinson's Disease [which he contracted in 2002] to shut me up." Childe Roland is not, though, without his fervent admirers, particularly among visual artists and certain Welsh-language llenorion; his performances and installations also beguile and delight many people with little prior experience of poetry, not least because, in their richly playful celebration of language and life, they are enormous fun.

Concrete poetry — which, admittedly, isn't everyone's bag of cement — can be simply defined as the pursuit of two of poetry's three main characteristics: the sound of the words in the ear and the look of the words on the page. It emphasises the physical characteristics of literature (form) above the emotional and intellectual ones (meaning). If the investigation is followed through to its logical end, the resulting work inclines towards music on the one hand and abstract visual art on the other, to such an extent that poetry's third characteristic, meaning, may be entirely absent — as in the cough and sneeze "poems" of the likes of Kurt Schwitters (1887-1948). If Childe Roland's experimentations have always been resolutely verbal, some other practitioners have detached themselves so completely from "the word" that they have ceased calling themselves poets. Bob Cobbing (1920-2002), for instance, the "father" of concrete poetry in Britain, described himself in his last years not as a poet but as a musician.

Such subversions of the perceived norms of poetry can upset people. Peter Finch was once invited to give an explanatory demonstration of concrete poetry to some budding writers at Neath Unemployed People's Centre. The group listened respectfully as Finch led them into the subject via Babylonian devil traps and Dizzy Gillespie's scat-singing; but when he started in on his own abstract vocal noises certain eyes widened with increasing incredulity.

"But this is meaningless!" exclaimed one of the lads.

"Precisely," came Finch's incendiary reply.

Debate between two of the lads, perched side by side on a settee, as to whether the "charlatan" should be shut down straight away or heard out and then denounced, reached such a fine point of discrimination that ultimately the matter could be decided only by "other means". A right-hook came flying at chin-height across the settee, to be returned by a left. Raining blows upon each other, the two lads ended up writhing on the floor; the settee was cast aside, tables and chairs were scattered, and others joined in the bardic fray. Thus ended abruptly what must be one of the most memorable performances of Finch's career.

Childe Roland's fidelity to the word and therefore to an element of meaning ensures that his productions are unlikely to be alienating affairs — indeed, they have the inviting allure of one of those Babylonian magic spirals. On the other hand, although a warmly congenial personality, his dealings with influential people such as editors and arts officials have not always been distinguished by their diplomacy, an uncompromising forthrightness in matters artistic tending to put backs up and raise barriers, doing little thereby to advance his cause. Then there are the unpromising associations with Victorian medievalism of his (seemingly) twee poodle of a pen-name that simply begs for a kicking from hostile critics (Peter Lord described it as "sugary" in a negative review).

He took that pen-name from Robert Browning's poem "Childe Roland to the Dark Tower Came" (1855), whose title — forming also the last words of the poem — is a line from the passage in *King Lear* in which Gloucester's son Edgar feigns madness as "poor Tom". Browning's poem describes a somewhat uneventful quest across a nightmarish wasteland, phrases such as "grey plain all round:/ Nothing but plain to the horizon's bound" doubtless chiming with Peter Meilleur's own obsessive quest, to cross the wilderness of the blank page. His pen-name has nothing, of course, to do with children, the word "childe" being a medieval term for an apprentice knight.

Born in Guildford, Surrey, in 1943, to a "thoroughly English" mother and a French-Canadian father who had joined the Canadian army to fight in the Second World War, he was raised in Canada, with a French-medium education and a bilingual home life. There were cultural tensions between his parents:

My mother just could not identify with the French Canadian side of life, whereas my father, although a federalist rather than a separatist, was a very proud French Canadian, always boasting about it, like me, because we were surrounded by English people. I knew from my experiences in Canada — with the English establishment constantly undermining French-speakers by institutionalising the view that their French was somehow not proper French, not the real thing — just what was happening in Wales when you met people who were apologetic about their Welsh, saying it wasn't as good as the Welsh that was spoken elsewhere.

Both parents were keen readers. "Dad used to quote poetry at me all the time, especially Longfellow and things like 'The Charge of the Light Brigade' and Robert Service's 'The Shooting of Dan McGrew'. At university, I was really high on Dylan Thomas, but I didn't realise then that Wales existed — isn't that appalling?"

He stumbled on Wales by accident. Having graduated in 1967 with a BA in French and English, he taught for a year in a French-medium high school, saving enough money for a trip to London in January 1969. "I was shocked by Britain. It was like Dinky Toy town. Everything was so small, and it was so cold, far colder than Canada, because no one had any central heating." A fascination with cathedrals saw him visiting a different cathedral city every weekend:

The last I visited was Chester Cathedral on March 8, my birthday. I didn't like the cathedral, a hellish red sandstone structure. I decided on a T-bone steak to cheer myself up

and then I got on a bus to this place I couldn't pronounce.
It was only when I got off the bus in Llangollen that I discovered
Wales — and, soon, its spectacularly beautiful
prosody. I was completely bowled over by it. I don't think
there's a poetry in the world that equals that.

But first he was to be bowled over by Welsh beauty of a different kind. Having rented a room in a Llangollen B&B, Peter attended a talk in the local library — by Nell Dunn, Angus Wilson, Christopher Logue and Margaret Drabble — and asked some questions. Word got back to the English teacher at Dinas Bran High School, via her pupils, that there had been this crazy Canadian at the reading. Keen to discover the crazy Canadian in person, the teacher presented herself at the B&B, where Peter was writing poetry in the front window — and within a matter of weeks they were married, with Sue wearing a wedding dress lent to her by the landlady of the B&B.

They spent the next ten years in Canada, raising three children, Emily (1970), Miranda (1971) and Tom (1973), and wintering over, when possible, in Wales — including a spell on the dole on Wrexham's Caia Park estate.

Peter's father had had such high expectations for his son that he had registered him at birth as "le Meilleur" — "the Best" rather than simply "Best" — but Peter managed eventually to drop the "le". While his parents were supportive of his literary ambitions, they would have liked to see him make good as a published author. But Peter was more "l'art pour l'art" than "l'art pour l'argent", the only money he made from his pen being the wages he earned as writer and editor, during the 1970s, in various government departments in Ottawa. His jobs included editing Edward B. Moogk's 444-page encyclopaedia of Canadian sound, writing articles for the *Labour Gazette,* scripting a film, and devising humorous handbooks such as *The Adventures of Inspector Phil de Loophole.* "They gave me some fun projects," he says, "and they were proud that I was their resident poet. Because I was interested in form, I made sure that my publications for the government looked good and had clarity. I insist on clear writing."

It intrigued him that from his commodious office in the National Library of Canada, on the Ontario side of the Ottawa river, he was able to encompass, in one expansive view, a significant cycle: he could look across Québec to the distant hills where the trees were felled that would be floated downstream as logs, to gather before the Eddy Company's pulp and paper mill, filling the Ottawa from bank to bank. "This mill," he says, "fed the paper-hungry civil service of the capital city and the paper-biased imagination of the concrete poet that I had become." It also provided the paper for his first collection of poetry, *the i sinfoni* (1971), which he printed on the presses of the *Labour Gazette*.

This sumptuously produced, 49-page book — his first outing as Childe Roland — is largely juvenilia, as he readily admits: it's sozzled with wordy, Dylanesque abstractions, formally incoherent, and peppered with typos and misspellings. But it embodies the germ of things to come: a fascination with huge amounts of white space, a delight in alliteration and word-play, restless experiments with patterns, shapes and breaking words across lines, the subversion of strict forms such as the sonnet, and some Welsh and French points of reference. It contains one wholly successful poem: at the top of the page, the letters of the word "rocker" describe a vertical crescent; at the bottom, you read the lines "with a quarter/moon/ you can make a". Perfect.

A much more successful project was his photographic collaboration *in octavo pace* (1976) which developed into a full collection of prose poems, published in a small edition by the poet's father as *six of clubs* (1997). This 48-poem sequence is an extended meditation on his obsession with the blank page, the materiality and the mystery of the writing surface:

I am almost overwhelmed by the published output of our
deciduous forests. I am further diminished by the knowledge
that the leaves of a book are manufactured by the
leaves of a tree. It is, like winter, with a blank page that I
counter this chlorophyllharmonic conspiracy of trees, having
learnt from the leaves of many a forest-felled book that
white contains all colours.

There were plans to publish a substantial selection of these impressive pieces in the 1992 edition of the Welsh Union of Writers' annual magazine *The Works*, but the Arts Council refused the Union adequate financial support to meet the production costs; *The Works* therefore collapsed, taking with it Childe Roland's hopes of a first "official" publication.

One of his first strictly concrete works was the controversial thesis he submitted for his MA at Carleton University, Ottawa in 1973. Having written a conventional academic thesis on concrete poetry, he decided against submitting it, in favour of a "thesis" which would itself be a concrete poem. Entitled *Allo Bell*, the "thesis" contains a handwritten introduction, without spaces between the words, followed by an "ode" of 100 pages — the minimum length for a thesis — of joined-up, handwritten "ℓ"s visually suggestive of a telephone cord, paying homage to Alexander Graham Bell, and reflecting the author's contention that one of the characteristics of literature is that it involves the spanning of space. "The poem should have been executed in copper wire, the physical material of Bell's invention," he wrote in his (untangled) foreword, "but on taking into account the introduction of papyrus as a writing material it was found that the two-dimensionality of the printed page was easier to carry than the plastic or three-dimensional rendition of the ode. The poem in its present state is an abstraction, a one-dimensional reduction of what it should have been..." It contains just three words: "alpha" at the beginning, "omega" at the end (as footnotes) — and the 100-page long central word, with its hundreds of "ℓ"s, "allo". This essay in maximised minimalism was too much for Carleton's more conservative academics, and he was refused the MA. "It split the department right down the middle," he says, "I lost friends over this book." The whole stressful episode was said later, in a feature by Marius Kociejowski in *PN Review* (vol. 29, no. 3), to have prompted "his one and only suicide attempt"; but in fact, says Peter, "I was drunk and I fell into a canal."

In 1976, he was invited to exhibit and to read in London, at a concrete poetry event organised by Bob Cobbing:

It was a shock, even though I had studied it. There was a bloke playing a bucket of water with a violin bow, people reading to record poetry in competition with themselves, all of them getting together in the garden of the Poetry Centre in Earls Court, growling and howling. Then on the tube, on our way to record something at the BBC, Bob Cobbing starts intoning some low, resonant note, joined then by Finch, and then by the rest of us — it blew my mind. I realised that at one end of the scale was verbal statements and at the other there was just noises.

Although he felt "too much of a coward to do what Cobbing did, just howling his abstract noises", it remains his conviction that if it is to be concrete poetry it has to be verbal.

Three years later, he was able at last to fulfill his dream — although not Sue's — of settling in Wales. There would be no turning back: he even brought with him his red granite tombstone, inscribed with a television screen and his signature, which is set into the wall of his back garden, waiting. (He watches a great deal of television; his favourite programme is *Blind Date*.)

Coming to live in Wales was the biggest mistake of my life.
We weren't rich, but we had it great in Canada. We arrived
here and had no money. It wasn't so much the financial
hardship that got to us but the isolation. In Ottawa, I had
access to all these wonderful libraries, but here there was
nothing. I didn't think, as I left Canada, that I had found myself
as a writer. Two years after I left Ottawa, the literary
scene there picked up. I should have been patient and waited.

The children were sent to Welsh-medium schools, becoming in time bilingual; Sue, returning to teaching, became the family's breadwinner, while Peter took on the role of house-husband. He, too, began learning Welsh, so that much of his output would be bilingual if not trilingual.

Most poets connect with their audiences through their books. If you have no books for sale, and declare yourself only through infrequent performances and home-made literary objects you are unlikely to attract much attention — and this has been Childe Roland's isolated lot. But what performances and what objects. Some performances are, in poetry terms, grand productions. The captivating show *Indigo*, for instance, which toured Wales in 1995, involved specially composed and pre-recorded music, the projection of visual images, dancers — and Peter reading his poetry (and, in Swansea, ignoring the blood seeping from a bare foot, caused by a splinter of glass). His fascination with the shearwaters on Ynys Enlli led to the composition of the 25-minute-long *Shearwater Oratorio Deryn Drycin* (2000), performed by a choir on the island itself. Based on a Morse-code "translation" of the Manx shearwater's enigmatic cry — dit-dit-dah-dit — the oratorio records some of the sights and sounds the bird encounters on its epic migration from Argentina to its breeding grounds on Enlli. It's full of auditory references, such as snippets of the shipping forecast as the bird enters British waters, and a Radio Cymru Welsh-language commentary as it arrives on Enlli. The Welsh and English phrases (to say nothing of the Latin) — all of which are voiced twice, to simulate the message being relayed from one bird to another — are sometimes equivalent, and at other points constructively divergent:

CLAMOR MEA	AD TE VENIAT
DIT-DIT-DAH-DIT	TANGO FOXTROT
DERYN DRYCIN	SHEAR-SHEARWATER
WYT TI'N DERBYN	HEAR MY CLAMOUR
BRON Y DONFEDD	DAYS ARE SHORTER
GALWAD ADREF	ROGER OVER
BRO GYNEFIN	UP THE TEMPO
DERYN DRYCIN	
YM MHORTH MADRYN	TANGO FOXTROT
TANGO OLAF	FEATHER FUSSY
PLU FFWDANNUS	
Y GYHYDNOS	EQUI-QUI-NOX
GREDDF YMWTHIO	BI-O-RYTH-THEMS
AR DRAWS ATSAIN	DIT-DIT-DAH-DIT
SGRECHAU'R HIRAETH	BARDSEY CALLING

In 2005, he staged his bilingual oratorio about the river Dee — rivers, particularly the St Laurent, the Ottawa and the Dee, being a constant source of inspiration. It was a major undertaking, involving the training of a 25-strong choir over a two-month period, without any funding. He complained to the Arts Council that "their lottery funding requirements are for accountants, not artists." This rigorously researched 147-line work begins:

DEE AND DEEPER	DYFRDWY'N DWYSÁU
DEE DIVA TO CAESAR	DYFRDWY DDWYFOL
DEE THE INSPIRATION	DYFRDWY DWYMYN AWEN
DEE DECLIVITIES	DYFRDWY DDWYFRON
DEE DILUVIAL	DYFRDWY LLWYNAU'R DILYW
DEE DEMONSTRATIVE	DYFRDWY DWYLO'R HYLIF
DEE THE ICE AGE GASH	DYFRDWY CLWYF OES YR IÁ
DEE THE EAVESDROP DRIP	DYFRDWY CYCHWYN CLEC
DEE DEPENDENT	DYFRDWY CYNLLWYNES
DEE THE ICICLE	DYFRDWY PIBONWY
DEE DEFROSTING	DYFRDWY CHWYS DIFEROL

But he doesn't need choirs, dancers, music and film to deliver a compelling reading. A sense of the impression made by just the man and his voice is communicated in an item in *The Absurd* (March 2009), the cultural online magazine for north Wales:

Childe... performed at a secret Absurd gig, in a barn, at a farm, on the side of a mountain... and what immediately strikes you, apart from his mischievous demeanour and shock of white hair, is that this poet is having fun... there is a feeling that you are with a man who cherishes life, who looks upon each day with wonder... Once he'd taken to the stage, Childe's 'The Fair' poem was received with roaring applause, and the end of the reading of "The Verb to Be" was met with raucous cheers and the demand for an encore... This was not an audience of the literary establishment; this was a party attended by over a hundred people... Childe's performance was animated, dynamic and vibrant; he stole the show.

His audiences have their favourites and make requests for such poems as "Children Chiefly", "The Same" (about Owain ab Urien and other history-haunting Owains), "Jones the Poem" and its Welsh-language doppelgänger, "Ifan y Gân Felan", or extracts from his exuberantly absurdist one-act play, *Ham and Jam*, in which Polonius asks incessantly "What are your plans for the future of the planet, my lord Hamlet, what are your plans?", receiving invariably a rhyming reply, such as "A wigwam, a hogan, a shaman in his shanty chanting amulets, ham and jam."

He works slowly and methodically at his compositions, some of which take many years to reach completion. With a sound poem, he normally starts by writing a traditional poem:

> *...to find a sound — rhyme or alliteration — that is connected*
> *in the minds of most people with the theme or subject*
> *that I am given to write about. Once I have found that*
> *sound, I consult all kinds of dictionaries to find all the words*
> *that contain the chosen sound. By some magic, all these*
> *words seem to define some aspect of the subject or theme.*
> *It is as if all the words are rushing to enter the poem, which*
> *seems to be writing itself, so to speak. Keeping control of*
> *this rush of words requires a lot of energy from me. There is*
> *no escape once the sound is invoked, for me or the audience.*
> *The sound poem contains some fillers, which may or may*
> *not echo the music of the chosen soundscape. These fillers*
> *are not to be spurned or misunderstood. They are the cement,*
> *the mortar between the lines.*

Peter Finch, in a curious poem about R.S. Thomas and Childe Roland called "The Light", touches on what distinguishes the latter's compositional procedures: "Childe Roland doesn't engage/language from the outside. He assembles it from/within."

Childe Roland has been a frequent, though generally unsuccessful, competitor in the National Eisteddfod, submitting his first contender for the Crown, the 700-line "Y Goleuadau", at Lampeter in 1984. While one of the judges, Dafydd Rowlands, dismissed the poem as "rhyw Dŵr Babel o nonsens" (some Tower of Babel of nonsense), another, Pennar Davies, gave it more hospitable consideration as "rhywbeth yn y canol rhwng cerdd goncrît fodernaidd ac ymgais i efelychu cyseinedd cyntefig yr hen ganu Gymraeg" (something between a modern concrete poem and an attempt to emulate the alliteration of early Welsh poetry). He had greater success with an exquisite celebration, in folded card and colour-coded threads, of the englyn, which was awarded £75 at the Porthmadog National Eisteddfod in 1987: it has four rows of threads, with the number of threads in each row corresponding to the number of syllables in each line of an englyn (10, 6, 7, 7); the order of the colours in each row of threads reflects the consonantal patterning of different kinds of cynghanedd.

His "literary objects", posters, cards and installations have had more exposure than his sound poetry. He has exhibited book art (with Picasso & co.) in Sardinia (the catalogue of that 1990 exhibition is *Il Librismo 1896-1990*) and at Swansea's Glynn Vivian Art Gallery (1995). Swansea is also the site of two permanent pieces, a set of six windows (with David Pearl) in a Gwalia housing scheme opposite High Street station, based on his "Elm" poem, and a one-word poem in stone, "youuuuuuuuuuu" (with Phil Chatfield), in Pier Street. However, most of his installations have been short-term interventions in the landscape, such as the prayer-wheel windmill garden created on Enlli (and at Alyn Waters Country Park, Wrexham) in 1999. This multi-coloured wind shrine, rooted in the fact that it is the wind that determines whether one may land on or leave Enlli, was fabricated by recycling plastic bottles washed ashore on the island; people were then invited to write a message, a prayer or a line of verse on a windmill.

Recycled packaging — and its iconography — forms the basis of many of his literary objects, which are first "published", for the most part, when he sends them to friends. I have a tea-chest's worth of such treasures: a balsa cheese carton with "CAWS LLENYDDOL" (literary cheese) written on the lid, and containing a square of yellow card folded into a triangle and riddled with holes; a cigar box containing a blue wave; a plastic spoon with a B-like heart carved in its bowl, and entitled "B-line love spoon", with a note explaining that it is "for hypoglycaemic lovers, so that they may go through the motions without harm"; a book with plain blue pages that opens to reveal a small bottle containing a minuscule paper ship; a coracle with paddle, to accompany his Dee poem, which is fashioned from the bottom of a bleach bottle, the creation's origins attested by inclusion of the bottle's label, because "a good scholar should always declare his sources to the public"; many caprices involving bar-codes, which he treats as akin to Ogham script — to name only a small selection. One's appreciation is often enriched by accompanying explanations, such as this elucidation of the "Boat Bottle Book":

This book-bound object combines the elements of a ship in a bottle with those of a message in a bottle, through the agency of a paper boat which, in the present circumstances, can be entertained as the ultimate message in a bottle, since the desire of all who are stranded is for a ship to rescue them. There is no need then for the message to be written; the folds that form the paper boat should suffice. However, if one were to undo these folds, one would be confronted with a blank page, perhaps the true content of the message. Moreover, the human body with its convoluted brain, the planet Earth with its various species, the universe with its spiral galaxies, are each like a bottle with a message inside. One cannot help wondering about the nature and character of the sender.

Thus, in the absence of any informed critical response to his work, Childe Roland has often felt obliged to provide his own. For the last ten years, he has been exploring the letter "B" and has produced, in association with that interrogation, his "VERB TO B", a seven-sonnet sequence of conjugations of the verb's present subjunctive mood. It's inspired both by William Blake's proposition that "what seems to be is to those to whom it seems to be" and by the subjunctive mood's expression of a wish or a condition which is contrary to fact. "Armed with this subversive tool," he says, "the poet constructs a hypothetical and yet familiar world where nothing is what it seems, where logic is undermined by its own rhyme and reasoning, where time is refuted with each heart beat, where matter does not matter, where the verb to be is actually the verb to love." The letter "B", which he renders as a stylised heart on its side, has not changed visually since its use as a hieroglyph depicting the floor plan of a two-room house; its Semitic name "Beth", meaning "house", appears in such place names as Bethel and Bethlehem. This heart-shaped "B" is the focus of dozens of three-dimensional objects known as the B-line series, because each distinctive design attempts to get to the heart — if not hearth — of the matter. A core set of them has been beautifully crafted on traditional wood-framed writing slates — "where people first learn to write the alphabet" — and provided with mounts to enable their easy display on a gallery wall. But no venue has shown the slightest interest in exhibiting these uniquely witty and illuminating creations.

In the three decades that Childe Roland has been making provocative art — and Welsh art at that — all manner of "Wales-based" pretenders have come and sometimes gone, piggy-backing to some modest renown on a culture whose surfaces they have barely scratched. He may have been ignored and disparaged, but he has forged resolutely onwards through the obscurity that Wales has lowered around him. There has been much debate as to the symbolism of Browning's *Dark Tower*; if, in Childe Roland's case, the tower might stand for a modicum of recognition, there have been signs lately that he might indeed be approaching its threshold. In 2001, he was surprised to find himself elected to the Welsh Academy. And this year (2009), he performed his poetry, to clamorous acclaim, to an audience of academics at the annual conference of the Association of Welsh Writing in English at Gregynog. Dr Matthew Jarvis, one of an exciting new generation of critics, declared in a subsequent blog: "Roland is an abundant and joyous poetic talent who I'd be delighted to have as a future National Poet of Wales. Petition, anyone?" But most significant of all, perhaps, was the phone call I received from Peter a week or so after that conference. "News flash," he said, "the Welsh version of my Dee poem, 'Dyfrdwy'n Dwysáu', has just been published in the spring issue of *Taliesin*. This is the first piece of work of mine to be published in Wales in a literary magazine." Wales may be acknowledging at last that this mere Childe of the avant-garde wilderness has long been, in fact, a "verray parfit, gentil knyght" of his craft and concrete art.

PLANET 195

Nigel's speech at his mother's 80th birthday

Friends, Family, Mary Gloria Ballantyne MacLeod – Mum
We're assembled this evening to celebrate an occasion which perhaps has taken us all a bit by surprise — not because we didn't think you'd make it this far (on the contrary) but because it's probably as startling to us as it is to you to think of you reaching such a venerable age while still, as ever, maintaining a remarkably alert and fresh attitude to life. It also means that the rest of us are notably advancing in age too, with all of your three offspring now the wrong side of 50.

Eighty years today, just as the General Strike was getting under way, you were born. From what I have read, it seems to have been a much warmer May than the one we are currently enduring, and I believe it went on to be a memorably warm summer. And that's the season, above all, that I associate you with — you picking bluebells with us as children, reading Beatrix Potter to us with the bedroom curtains billowing in the warm July air, riding with us on side-saddle, you taking us down to Horton for long idyllic seaside days, inviting us to help you carry the tea to the men in the fields at harvest time, and you sometimes driving the tractor to them. Then there were great dramas, like the time Martyn took your wedding ring for a walk around the estate and lost it, seemingly for ever — but it was found again after a massive search. Then there was the much more significant drama of Carey's arrival on the scene — which you managed very cannily, forestalling any possibility of us two boys feeling left out of proceedings, by acting dumb and asking our advice as to how to how best to go about bathing this baffling little bundle.

You have resisted settling into any of the clichés of advanced years. You have always been an individual with a notable independence of mind, and someone to whom we have all been able to come in times of trouble or uncertainty — to receive the benefit of advice informed by wide reading in current and social affairs and by careful consideration of the various pros and cons. After lunch with you recently, in the car on the way home, Branwen remarked, 'You know, Gaga is a very sensible person, isn't she?'

You have also been unstintingly and hugely generous over the years. If you've been able — with money, time, energy, ideas — to lighten anyone's load, you have always been pleased to do so. And it's not just family members who have been the beneficiaries of your largesse. I remember umpteen quiet kindnesses to all sorts of people, from the invitation to Christmas dinner to someone with nowhere else to go, to the very considerable cheque despatched regularly to charities such as Oxfam.

Just about anyone, by definition, can do common sense. Much more productive is the kind of thoughtful uncommon sense that you have been able to reach for at difficult times — and indeed you've had your share of difficult times, from marital troubles and daunting financial hardship, through Niney and Pa's increasingly distressing and demanding last years, to the loss of dear friends — to say nothing of the aches and quite severe pains of recent health troubles.

The one constant, through all of life's vicissitudes, has been your sense of humour. You have never allowed life's harder blows to get the better of you, and have faced all of life's challenges with courage and resourcefulness on the one hand, and an unfailing sense of humour on the other — a sense of humour, of course, being a wonderful way of getting things in perspective. Often that humour has been decidedly wacky, larpike warpen yarpou tarpaught arpus harpow tarpo sparpeak arparp larpanguarpage — darpo yarpou rarpemarpembarper tharpat?

I think most of our friends, when we were teenagers, felt that you were not like other mothers — by which they probably meant you were not the conformist or superior kind of parent that children found difficult to relate to, but someone they could talk to and have fun with, even if some of our more conservative pals found you, shall we say, somewhat eccentric. But you have always quietly revelled, I think, in being a little off centre — which has expressed itself, for instance, in your painting of 'muriels' on the kitchen wall in 1960s and, just lately, in your outlandish ambition to go bungee jumping and also to take trip, like some queen of circus aeronautics, standing on the wings of a biplane. Not, perhaps, such an impossible caper for someone who only a couple of years ago went paragliding. But your doctor, we were relieved to hear, cautioned against such antics. There seems, though, to be no objections to your taking flight in a helicopter at Fairwood — although I don't think we should mention this to the good citizens of Killay and Three Crosses and other places under the flightpath.

In conclusion, I know I speak for all of us in thanking you for being a wonderful daughter, mother, grandmother and friend, but, more than that, for being simply yourself — an unfailingly unique, loving and much loved human being. We salute more birthday meals like this to come.

23 May 2006

Mary Gloria Ballantyne MacLeod
(known to her grandchildren as gaga)
23 May 1926 - 30 July 2012

Older than my dad

Broadcast on John Peel's Home Truths

He died on December 11, 1971, just six months after his forty-eighth birthday. I, the eldest of his three children, was twenty-two. It's been a date to remember, but a short while ago another date crept up on me out of time's ticking shadows, the moment at which, turning forty-eight and a half, I found myself overtaking my father. If my luck holds for ten or twenty years more, I could be the grey and balding paterfamilias that my youthful old man never made it to be.

The ancient Celts believed that no one truly died, you simply shuffled off into the Celtic underworld, and could return from time to time to mingle with the living. And that, sometimes, is how it seems in our dreams, when the dead come back and wander round inside our heads, insisting by sheer force of presence, and the persuasiveness of a conman, that surely there's been some absurd mistake, they never died, how could anyone have imagined such a thing? For years after his death my dad would pay nocturnal visits, urging on me all manner of resurrectionist scams, until, seeing through his resourceful yarns, I'd have to take him regretfully by the arm and say 'Dad, mun, you're dead, now lie back down, and leave me alone'. Then I'd wake up, and yes Dad would be dead.

But with an afterlife in the memories of the living, the dead rarely leave us alone for long, and as far as most of mine are concerned, they've got a key to the house and can wander back in whenever they want. These encounters can take place in various forms — dreams, recollections, family chats or, in dad's case, a poem. He was a great horseman, so what better, I thought, than to couch the moment of my overtaking him in terms of a horse race, with him on my mother's black-maned mare and me astride a certain grand if mildly delinquent bay. We were never great talkers, my dad and me, but we managed to communicate least dysfunctionally, I suppose, when we were out together on horseback. And there were some things now, approaching forty-eight and a half, that I wanted to talk to him about — not least my fears that somehow I'd fail to overtake him, and my horse would take a fatal stumble at the off.

I wanted this race to be not so much a reckoning as a reconciliation, a working through and settling of differences — a celebration, finally, in spite of all that had divided us as I floundered towards manhood through my adolescent and what would be his last years. There had indeed been furlongs between us. What about, Dad, the anglicising public school so-called education that brought a happy childhood to such a ragged end, and did its best to turn a boyish Taff into an English toff? What about the foxhunting? What about that penchant for the Tory-voting hang-n-flog-em shires? Against his Brylcreemed mohawk I had raised a revenge of tresses sufficient to thatch an army of Guevaras. Against the alleged music of Sir Harry Lauder I had turned, full-volume, the orgasmitudes of Hendrix. I didn't want to be a farmer, Dad.

Then, neck and neck, through the months of his heart's perplexed liberation after the release — for them both — of my parents' divorce, we found mutual forgiveness for perceived shortcomings, found in each other the boy and the man. Able at last to see our matters of division from the other's point of view, we could raise our glasses — his a Scotch, mine a Guinness — to the future.

Death, though, had another plan. To the black wart on his wrist that was *not* a wart, my father took an agricultural knife, sporing cancer before long through the whole of his body. He was dead within months. 'So young,' said mourner after head-shaking mourner. It was, I remember feeling, daylight, scorched-earth robbery.

But back to the race, and after twenty-seven years of catching up,

the plashy nostrils of my lathered mount are panting down my
father's skeletal neck, and he'll be lost any second in flying hoof-
scoops of earth and grass — unless, unless, yes, c'mon, Dad, gimme
your hand, I gotcha: leap! Leap up behind me! And we're riding on
together in galloping tandem, my dad forever aged forty-eight and a
half, and me, perhaps — we'll see — getting old for the pair of us.

BBC Radio 4, October 28 2000

Humberto Gatica and Nigel Jenkins
Afterword

The Sand Garden — El Jardin de Arena

Following 1973's military coup in Chile, the largest community of Chilean exiles in Wales settled in Swansea — which, for much of the nineteenth century, thanks to Swansea's world dominance of the copper trade, had been more or less the economic capital of Chile, the prime source of Swansea's ore. Among the eighty or so Chileans exiled in Swansea — few of whom, initially, would have been aware of the largely forgotten Swansea-Chile connection — was the poet and photographer Humberto Gatica.

Humberto, who arrived in Swansea with his wife Gabriela in 1975, was born in 1944 in the southern village of Huellahue, Panguipulli, in the territory of the indigenous Huilliche people — a region of rain, mountains, farms and forests not unlike parts of Wales. The presence of both geographies, although neither of them is named, is palpable in many of the poems in this collection. Like Wales, Chile is a land of poets: kick up any stone in Chile, it is said, and you'll find a poet lurking there. A poet born not far away from Humberto's birthplace was Pablo Neruda (1904-73), one of the greatest Spanish-language poets of the twentieth century, whose poems were an inspiration to the carpenter's son from Huellahue. Humberto's first efforts, at the age of thirteen or fourteen, were more prayer than poem: 'I come from a very religious family, and I liked the rhythm of the prayer.' But in the regional capital of Valdivia, where, aged about fifteen, he studied to become an electrician, he found poetry in its libraries that excited his interest. There was also the custom in his village of gathering on Sundays to drink and chat. 'They'd get a little drunk, then they'd start to sing and recite poetry — dramatic poetry and poetry made out of the little things of everyday life. My curiosity was aroused: how to write poems about these little things?'

Not surprisingly, the haiku and its minimalist procedures would exert a considerable influence on this maker of slender, pared-down, carefully observed lyric constructions. (He writes haiku not in Spanish but in English: 'when I try to translate haiku in Spanish, the line is too long.') Invariably short and succinct, his poems are nevertheless the fruit of painstaking, regular craftsmanship. 'I get up around five every morning, and work for about two and a half hours on my poetry before I go to the university', (since 1987, he has taught photography at what is now Swansea Metropolitan University). 'Maybe I don't write more than a line or manage more than finding just one word. But I have to attend to my poetry every day, and feel guilty if I do not.'

The poems in this collection, with their theme of enforced exile and the struggle to adapt to life in a foreign land, are the fruits of harsh political happenstance. A supporter of democratically elected President Allende, Humberto was working on a community arts programme in the mountains when Pinochet and his generals crushed the Popular Unity government's daring socialist experiment. Humberto was among the thousands indiscriminately rounded up, jailed, beaten and — in the worst cases, tortured, mutilated, killed or 'disappeared'. After ten months in prison, during which he was subjected to brutal interrogations, a group of French artists and intellectuals managed to secure his release. Friends advised Humberto and Gabriela to flee the country. They settled for a while in Mendoza, Argentina, until the political situation in that country worsened, when they sought asylum in Europe. Towards the end of 1975, they arrived in Swansea; here they have remained, apart from an interlude in Mozambique, where they worked on a community project. Their three children, one of whom died in infancy, were born in Swansea and Cardiff and are, of course, citizens of Wales (or 'British subjects', as officialdom would have it).

Although photography has been Humberto's bread and butter, and he loves teaching the subject, poetry has always been his first priority. The two arts nevertheless inform each other. 'What they have in common, for me, is simplicity and an emphasis on the sense of beauty. Out of a great sense of solemnity in my village, comes this desire to make beauty.'

Although a long way now from Huellahue, his native locality continues to play on his imagination. 'I still have my village on my back. It's difficult to dissociate myself from that experience.' He is haunted by 'the music / of my rains / and / my broken / landscape', a haunting made the more poignant (in the context of exile) by his use of imported touchstones — such as fireflies and lime trees — as similes and metaphors.

The wounds of exile, as these poems attest, are not easily assuaged. But surviving the trauma may have much to do with the place of refuge; Humberto is glad that, largely by accident, he and his family ended up in Swansea. The city, whose geography reminds many Chileans of Valparaiso, 'is more than a city,' he says: 'it's a collection of villages.' He is delighted that this, his first collection of poetry (although he has published many poems in magazines), is being published in Swansea.

HAFAN BOOKS JANUARY 2008

192

Remembering Nigel

John Barnie recalls good times with Nigel Jenkins
— poet, essayist, editor, musician and friend,
who died in January.

— You mean, you've sold my hat — twice!

Nigel Jenkins, Twm Morys, Iwan Llwyd and I were in Bergan Brothers, gents' outfitters, in Syracuse, NY. We were in Syracuse to perform as Y Bechgyn Drwg/The Bad Boys, our bilingual blues and poetry band, but that afternoon we discovered Bergans, a tailor's unlike any in Wales catering mostly, I think, for the black community. There was rack on rack of suits in cerise, kingfisher blue, tangerine and lime green, with jackets available in three lengths, 'lounge', 'matinée' and 'opera', matinée being down to the knees, opera down to the ankles, all in shiny polyester.

As Twm weighed up a canary-yellow suit, matinée length, with matching homburg (he decided in the end that Gwynedd wasn't ready), Nigel paid for a black, broad-brimmed hat, which he put down to browse further among the rainbow colours of the store. While he was doing this, one of the Bergan Brothers sold the hat a second time to the 'Bishop of Manhattan', as he informed Nigel with a slightly amused smile when the latter discovered it was missing — the Bishop being an oldish black man I had noticed in the shop earlier, pastor, I suspect, of a store-front church.

— Have you got *another* one?

— No.

With the help of Mr Bergan, however, Nigel rooted around and found a replacement to his satisfaction, matching it up with a matinée-length black suit, which from then on he wore when

Nigel Jenkins, John Barnie, Iwan Llwyd and Twm Morys

performing with Y Bechgyn, and later with Llaeth Mwnci Madoc/Madoc's Moonshine, a trio he and I formed with Iwan. With his imposing physical presence and harmonicas slung round his waist in a specially designed belt, he might have stepped out of a 1940s Western. But Nigel was a fine harmonica player who achieved a rich, sonorous tone in the amplified style of Chicago bluesmen like Walter Horton and James Cotton.

Performing with Y Bechgyn was fun; we enjoyed one another's company, and enjoyed mixing poetry with music which included Twm and Iwan's songs in Welsh as well as blues. There was lots of wine and a certain unpredictability in performance which could be stimulating even if it got us in trouble now and then. (We are probably still personae non gratae at Keble College, Oxford.)

The first group Nigel and I formed was The Salubrious Rhythm Co. with Swansea jazz pianist Jen Wilson. That too could be unpredictable. Performing at the 'Wales Week' in Brussels, the PA system was so poor and the hubbub of voices in the pub where we were playing so loud that I couldn't hear my guitar or Jen's piano and kept time by watching her tap her foot. Only Nigel's harmonica reached me distantly, bounced off the far end of the room. The gig was a wash-out and in the end we just stopped.

There were consolations on that trip, though. It was bitterly cold in Brussels and we were not dressed for it. With two days to go before our flight back to Wales, we found a corner pub-café and, after wandering around the city in the morning, spent our time there, working our way through the bar's list of velvety Belgian monastery beers between ordering lunch and supper. When on our last day Nigel, who spoke French picked up in his grape-harvesting days in southern France, told the landlady we were leaving that afternoon, she gave us lunch for free.

Nigel was not a singer, but his full, rounded bass voice made him a wonderful reader of his own poems. 'Oh I wish someone would bottle your voice!' an admiring woman told him after one performance.

As well as being a bluesman of course he was many other things. For some years he worked as English-language editor of *The Encyclopaedia of Wales* and this added immensely to his already considerable knowledge of Wales and its two cultures. Sometimes, driving with him to a performance, he would invent a character for himself — the nineteenth-century antiquary — 'Cyclopaedic Jenkins', and we would stop off, perhaps at Cilmeri where he would take me over the battle ground where Llywelyn ap Gruffudd lost his life. Another time we stopped at Tryweryn. It was a summer day and butterflies flew around us as we walked across the boulder-strewn retaining wall of the dam. We talked about Capel Celyn and the drowning of a community that brought Mudiad Amddiffyn Cymru into being and galvanised Welsh political life. Looking at the placid surface of the lake, a stranger could not guess any of this, but it seemed cold and alien if you knew. He told me water from the reservoir was released periodically so people could play at white water canoeing in the stream below.

After the Encyclopaedia was published he became a member of the English Department at Swansea University teaching creative writing. Perhaps because he knew my views on the creative writing movement this was something we rarely discussed, though when he became director of the MA programme and enmeshed in administration, I enjoyed emails in which he projected another of his fantasy personae, the 'Fat Controller'.

Nigel was a politically committed poet in the tradition of Harri Webb who he admired; he wrote about the drowning of the valley in 'The Ballad of Cwm Tryweryn'. He was not afraid of controversy and must have expected the furore that followed the publication of his flyting on the death of George Thomas, 'An Execrably Tasteless Farewell to Viscount No', when it appeared in the *New Welsh Review*. Walking in downtown Swansea next day, he told me, he was overtaken by a battered car that screeched to a halt. Two tough-looking young men got out and strode toward him. He expected trouble, but they just shook his hand vigorously, got back in the car and drove off.

His poetry also celebrated life in the raw, as in 'Byzantium in Arfon', where a group of American students are exposed to Saturday-night Caernarfon:

In the Black Boy a jilted bonker
whines at his mount as she leaves with someone else.
'Look,' she shouts back, 'Rwy'n i ffycio fo heno
a chdi y-ffycyn-fory.'

He always performed this poem with Y Bechgyn Drwg and did so with gusto, certainly for the bawdy, but also because, as the poem goes on to explain, Caernarfon 'is by now the Welshmost town in

Wales'. On Saturday nights it might be full of 'the blitzpop blasting from disco-bars, / the vomit-falls, the can-kicked crowded streets, / fist, yell, or yowl', but it is a celebration of 'whatever is youthful, loud and Welsh', and that is what counted for Nigel. He embraced all aspects of Welsh life, savoury and otherwise.

He was also a member of Plaid Cymru and a committed republican — you wouldn't find him standing in line at Buckingham Palace to bow before the Queen of England, as some Welsh poets did recently.

As a poet he could be a fine lyricist, an aspect of his work that found expression especially in his two collections of haiku, *Blue* and *O for a Gun*:

at dawn, as at dusk,
the windows of Swansea
take fire and burn

Latterly, although he produced the occasional haiku, a form about which he was extremely knowledgeable, the poetry dried up. We discussed this at times. The inspiration had simply gone, and Nigel was too honest a writer to delude himself that it was still there by producing second-rate pastiches 'in the manner of', which it is too easy for poets to do. This was a cause for regret on his part, but he transferred his energies into researching and writing two books for Seren's Real Wales series, *Real Swansea* and its sequel *Real Swansea Two*. These were partly a spin-off from his years working as an editor on *The Encyclopaedia of Wales*, work that developed his love of the peopled landscapes of Wales and honed his eye for telling detail (something equally evident in the haiku). The books were popular. We were in a pub one lunchtime when a man approached Nigel enthusiastically at the bar. I assumed they knew each other, but Nigel had never seen him before. The man had recognised him and wanted to say how much he'd enjoyed *Real Swansea.*

At the time of his death he was working on a third volume in the series, *Real Gower*, and last July he took Helle Michelsen and me on two long walks on the peninsula. To stay with Nigel in his flat in Mumbles was to start the day with one of his legendary breakfasts. All four gas rings on the stove would be blazing, as well as the grill and the oven as he juggled pans with bacon, fried eggs, tomatoes, mushrooms, and laverbread rolled in crushed oats, while toasting bread, warming plates and rustling up cans of strong coffee. Breakfast might be prepared for anything up to four or five guests with a deceptive ease, all the dishes ready for the plate at the same time.

Those were warm sunny days last July and Nigel took us along lanes and down tracks some of which must have been known to few others than himself. His passion for Gower, where he was brought up, and his intimate knowledge of its layered history meant he was the perfect guide, whether we stopped at Arthur's Stone, the Neolithic burial site on the ridge of Cefn Bryn, or made our way along a path overgrown with gorse and bracken to Vernon Watkins' memorial stone above Hunts Bay. He also knew which pubs had the best beer and several stops were inevitable.

On the second day we were joined by Nigel's partner, Margot Morgan, and descended the cliff path to Bacon Hole. The cave had, he explained, been occupied during the Iron Age, but it must have been as a bolt hole in times of emergency because it would not have been a pleasant place to live. When Nigel shone a torch on the walls it was as if they were covered with a myriad milky pearls — the light refracted from water droplets seeping out of the limestone. Delicate liverworts crowded wet boulders near the entrance; even at the back of the cave where there was a permanent gloom, algae thrived on the dark, wet surface of the rock.

Early on the first evening, Nigel, Helle and I went to Pepper's Wine

Bar across the road from his flat. I had been there last with Nigel and Iwan Llwyd when we were rehearsing for a performance as Llaeth Mwnci Madoc and we had sat on the bar's tiny terrace drinking white wine, Iwan's drink of choice. Iwan had died three years earlier, only fifty-two, and we were there now to raise a glass in his memory.

After a long day's walk exploring Gower, we were ready to relax, enjoying the cool wine as Pepper's began to fill with people dropping by on their way home from work. There was that sense of ease and slowness at the end of a summer's day when it seems as though you have all the time in the world. You don't, of course, and as I recall that evening, on the last time we ever met, I remember another of Nigel's haiku:

how many of the dead,
as I climb these old stairs,
do I pass coming down?

PLANET 214

Obituaries

In memory of Nigel Jenkins

Professor M. Wynn Thomas

'Nigel Jenkins: Gower poet.' How grotesquely inadequate an epithet, when used in a journalistic context. Yet how otherwise apt. For Nigel was nothing if not a grounded person, who fiercely stood his ground. And that ground was Gower, the beautiful peninsula extending its fragile length out into the wild western waters, which provided him with a vantage point not only on his beloved Wales in its infuriating entirety, but on the wider world and indeed the cosmos. It was, so his friend Stevie Davies movingly testifies, when bathing off Gower's beaches he best felt able to immerse himself in the oceanic immensities of the universe.

And then there was the intricate chain of Gower bays — smugglers' coves of old, with their stories of wreckers, rum, and illicit dealings under cover of darkness. Nigel was in his element there. With his strong frame, his beard of piratical cut, his sexily deep voice, his satiric bent, there was something of the buccaneer, the rebel, the outlaw about Nigel always.

He had been made such partly by his early experiences. Sent to private schools across the border to be 'civilized' into an Englishman, he came 'home' shamefully, defiantly Welsh, and his whole life was spent trying to reclaim in its fullness that of which, he felt, he'd been early deprived. Most of all, of course, the language. Having learnt it, he placed his talents at its disposal, his translations serving to bring together the two cultures of his broken-backed Wales.

After Wales, his life-long love was the USA, to whose recklessly innovative poetry he was first introduced at Essex University in the turbulent sixties. Then came his colourful but brutal initiation into the contrasting realities of 'mainstream' US culture, when he toured the States of the late Vietnam era with a circus company.

By the time I met him, in the early seventies, all this was behind him, as was the period in journalism that provided him with skills on which he continued to draw to the end. With me he wanted to study the poetry of Meic Stephens, a figure who fascinated Nigel because he saw in him a promising poet who had 'abandoned' his talent. And why? In order (or so Nigel felt) to become an arts administrator, dedicated to the development of the infrastructure necessary for the cultural survival of a small 'stateless' nation in the modern world. While respecting the achievement, Nigel's response was typically dissenting. He became 'shop steward' of a Welsh Union of Writers intended as a check on the growing powers of the Welsh Arts Council.

Now, forty years later, I can see that in Meic Stephens Nigel foresaw the dilemma he would himself face: how to protect the 'inner rebel' from which authentic writing (and most particularly poetry) could alone come while devoting one's energies to the collective good of one's country and its people. That such a balancing act was possible was proved, for him, in the ample flesh of Harry Webb, himself proud of his Gower stock, whose day job was that of a respected borough librarian while in his roistering night life he presided, with Falstaffian gusto, over raucous sessions of 'poems and pints' designed to educate the post-industrial masses in their own lost history.

Education: that, too, was eventually to be Nigel's chosen medium and milieu. But first he was a writer, and foremost a poet. He deliberately adopted such roles as that of the *bardd gwlad* (poet to a locality and its communities) and *bardd llys* (poet of more grand, formal public occasions). In the latter capacity he regularly recited tongue-in-cheek at Swansea University's graduation ceremonies his paean of praise to the Swansea he so passionately loved even while lavishly cursing its philistinism and English provincialism. And then there was his tireless work to enable local writers to make their silenced voices heard, and the 'civic art' that saw his poems pave streets and leave their mark permanently on buildings.

Nigel laughed at the idea of a poet developing a preciously singular 'voice.' His poems were deliberately miscellaneous in character, because he wanted them to convey not only the multifariousness of human experience but also the range of different collectivities that constituted any human society. The devotion to Wales given such monumental expression in the great *Encyclopaedia* he edited with self-consuming energy and devotion never blinded him to the terrible shortcomings of the country and its easily complacent people. In a classic, prize-winning study, he tracked down the history of the Welsh missionaries in the Khasia hills of the Indian sub-continent, highlighting the white colonial aspects of an epic project that nevertheless left a legacy of blessings. Naturally drawn to the 'underside' of his native city, he brought a detective's zeal and a reporting journalist's unsparing eye in his *Real Swansea* volumes to those parts of the city its primly respectable citizens never reached. And then there was his love-song to his Gower, in the form of a magnificent portrait-essay of the peninsula, from the deep history of its ancient rocks to the packaged beauty of its present.

Having developed, in tandem with the Welsh-language poet Menna Elfyn, a visionary creative writing course at Trinity College, Carmarthen, Nigel eventually came home to Swansea, where he worked alongside Stevie Davies (and later several other close colleagues). Together, they established another pioneering creative writing course uncompromisingly dedicated to honouring the integrity of writing as both craft and vocation while valuing and nurturing the differing talents of students. He was a wonderful teacher.

'Nigel was much loved,' a colleague remarked movingly when he heard of his passing. Yes, much loved even though he never compromised his beliefs or diluted his principles in order to please. He remained a maverick to the last — quietly, courteously but wickedly sabotaging every administrative and bureaucratic attempt to bring him to heel. A free spirit, he somehow seemed most at home on his bike, self-propelled, independent, unconfined, comrade of wind and weather.

Ffarwél fy annwyl ffrind. A boed iti fwynhau yn y byd nesaf gwmni llawen y criw afreolus o awduron, a cherddorion ac artistiaid yr oedd dy enaid erioed yn ei chwennych.

CREW - CENTRE FOR RESEARCH INTO THE
ENGLISH LITERATURE AND LANGUAGE OF WALES,
SWANSEA UNIVERSITY
MONDAY, 3 FEBRUARY 2014

In Memory of Nigel Jenkins

Welsh Writers' Trust

Nigel Jenkins was a much-loved and internationally renowned writer. It is with deep sadness — felt and expressed both by those who knew him personally and those who did not — that 2014 has played witness to his passing.

Born in 1949 in Gorseinon, near Swansea, Nigel Jenkins studied Literature and Film at the University of Essex, after first embarking upon stints as a newspaper reporter in England and, briefly, as a circus-hand in America. However in 1976 Jenkins returned home to the country of his birth, where he promptly set about learning Welsh.

Once settled in Swansea Jenkins remained there, both writing and teaching, for the rest of his life. He gained renown as a performance poet, notable for his deep bass voice and good humour. And up till January this year, when he passed away aged 64 from pancreatic cancer, Jenkins also taught at Swansea University, where he acted as the director of the Creative Writing programme.

Beyond the borders of the classroom, Jenkins also inspired students and aspiring writers with his own work; work which addressed political issues largely from a left-wing, Nationalist angle, and often with a satirical bent.

Jenkins' interest in Wales and issues of Welsh identity was also evident in the projects he supported; among them, the Welsh Writer's Trust, and the Welsh Union of Writers, for which he acted as the first Secretary. Jenkins also co-edited the Academi's *Encyclopaedia of Wales*.

The list of published works Jenkins leaves behind him, as both an editor and writer, is impressively varied, featuring poetry, prose, travel fiction, criticism, and even two plays, both chronicling the lives of two other great Welshmen; *Strike a Light!*, about Dr William Price, the pioneer of cremation, and *Waldo's Witness*, about the Welsh-language pacifist poet Waldo Williams.

Yet, despite his prolific list of publications, Jenkins never sheltered behind the page, or the teacher's desk. He was an active figure in his community, promoting the written word wherever he could. He contributed to television documentaries, toured with blues and poetry bands, and composed site-specific poetry for his hometown.

Now Jenkins' poetry can be found engraved in stone, steel, and glass throughout the streets of Swansea. One installation on Christina St, which retrospectively seems to speak poignantly for Jenkins' life, reads: ''Came for a day — setlo am oes' (stayed a lifetime)''.

Throughout his lifetime Jenkins received great critical acclaim, and several notable awards, including the John Tripp Spoken Poetry Award in 1998, and the Wales Book of the Year Prize in 1995, for his travel book *Gwalia in Khasia*. Jenkins also drew attention and notoriety for producing the first ever book of haiku poetry from a Welsh publisher, and for his translations of modern Welsh poetry, which have appeared in publications all over the globe. Indeed, Jenkins has been translated into numerous languages and reprinted in just as many countries.

In kind, his passing has been mourned and his life celebrated by many. His funeral, which took place in St Mary's Church, Pennard, was simultaneously broadcast in the nearby community hall, where hundreds of mourners had gathered. Jenkins was then buried in the graveyard of St Mary's, joining the company of esteemed poets Vernon Watkins and Harri Webb.

Jenkins leaves behind his wife Delyth Evans and their two daughters, Branwen and Angharad, an impressive and versatile body of work, and a legacy in the minds of his readers and students that

207

will not be diminished by his passing.

He was a master of his form, into which he showed great insight, as can be seen in his poem 'Where Poems Came From' in which Jenkins claims his poems came 'behind my back/they talked to me/though I heard no words/their coming was not to do with words/It was in the laughter of dogs/way across the snow'.

Not only did Jenkins teach Creative Writing to his own students, his poetry is still used as exemplar work in Creative Writing programmes across Wales. Reading it, it is clear to see why.

Another poem by Jenkins, in a similar vein, asserts that poetry should not be 'fog and tricks/but accuracy and magic'. In his lifetime, and in his writing, Jenkins both articulated this ideal and lived it; setting a standard for young writers all across Wales to aspire to, and be inspired by.

He brought poetry to life, in a network of classrooms and streets mapped out across Wales. His work and life will be recalled in the legacy of these words; words for which now we can only thank him, and use to remember him by.

Nigel Jenkins Obituary

Noel Witts

My cousin, the writer Nigel Jenkins, who has died aged 64 after suffering from pancreatic cancer, taught himself Welsh and went on to become a leading literary figure in Wales. He was born into an Anglo-Welsh family in Gower, the son of an auctioneer and farmer, and immersed himself in the language. He was also known as a performance poet, captivating audiences with his deep bass voice.

After attending Dean Close School in Cheltenham and studying at Essex University, he started his career as a journalist in Leamington Spa, but in time returned to Swansea and learned Welsh. He taught creative writing at the University of Wales, Lampeter, and was ultimately director of the creative writing course at Swansea University.

His first publication in 1972 was followed by numerous poetry collections, including *Song and Dance* (1981) and *Hotel Gwales* (2006), the travel book *Gwalia in Khasia* (1996), a study of Welsh missionaries in India, for which he won a national award, *Ambush* (1988), and a volume of essays and articles, *Footsore on the Frontier* (2001).

Nigel was elected as a bard to the Gorsedd Beirdd Ynys Prydain in 1998. In 2007 he was a co-editor of the massive *Welsh Academy Encyclopaedia of Wales* (2007), now a standard reference work. He also wrote two books in the Seren Books Real series: *Real Swansea One* and *Real Swansea Two*, which, as classics of psychogeography in the making, delved far below the surface of the city. His *Real Gower* was left unfinished at the time of his death.

Nigel was married to Delyth Evans, a folk harpist, who survives him, as do their daughters, Branwen and Angharad, who is a member of the Welsh contemporary folk group Calan.

He spent much time encouraging others but he also had a ribald side. His poem "Some Words for English Viceroys, Rugby Players, and Others, in Abuser-Friendly English to Help Them Con Televiewers That They Can Sing the Welsh National Anthem" was inspired by the sight of the then secretary of state for Wales, John Redwood, failing to convince with his rendition of Hen Wlad Fy Nhadau (Land of our Fathers).

Nigel suggested a phonetic version for non-Welsh speakers:

"My hen laid a haddock, one hand oiled a flea
Glad farts and centurions, threw dogs in the sea
I could stew a hare here and brandish Dan's flan
Don's ruddy bog's blocked up with sand
Chorus
Dad! Dad! Why don't you oil Auntie Glad?
Can whores appear in beer bottle pies
O butter the hens as they fly!"

THE GUARDIAN NEWSPAPER - 18 MARCH 2014

Nigel Jenkins: Politically engaged and outspoken poet whose work often landed him in trouble with the officials he meant to offend

Meic Stephens

Jenkins: *"it is my good fortune," he said, "to work in a country which, unlike its neighbour to the east, has a tradition of poetry as a social art"*

Of all Welsh poets writing in English, Nigel Jenkins was one of the most politically engaged and outspoken. His views and actions often got him into hot water.

In 1988 he was jailed for seven days for refusing to pay a £40 fine imposed after a protest outside the American airbase in Brawdy, in Pembrokeshire. He had cut the perimeter fence as part of CND's Operation Snowball, a campaign aimed at persuading the government to vote in favour of multilateral disarmament. "I consider it my duty as a Welshman and an internationalist," he told reporters, "to do all in my power to end the continuing presence on Welsh soil of American and British nuclear bases." In 1987 he co-edited the anthology *Glas-Nos* for CND Cymru.

Jenkins believed, unlike Auden, that poetry could make things happen, especially in Wales, where poets are often called upon to write verse that inspires the community to take action against overweening officialdom. His poems were meant to offend, and offend they often did. When his "Execrably Tasteless Farewell to Viscount No" appeared in *The Guardian* in 1997, he was pilloried for satirising George Thomas, the recently deceased Commons Speaker who had been prominent in the No camp during the

Devolution campaign. It was the vitriolic language that raised most hackles: "white man's Taff ... may his garters garrotte him ... the Lord of Lickspit, the grovelsome brown-snout and smiley shyster whose quisling wiles were the shame of Wales..."

Jenkins courted controversy whenever possible. Commissioned (with Menna Elfyn and David Hughes) in 1993 to write site-specific poems for the refurbished city centre in Swansea, his native place, he jumped at the opportunity to give poetry the public profile he believed it should have in the lives of the people: "It is my fortune to work in a country which, unlike its neighbour to the east, has an unbroken tradition of poetry as a social art."

But most of the one-liners such as "Remember tomorrow" inscribed on benches, flagstones, walls, bollards and signposts, were obliterated or removed — not by vandals or hostile citizens but by council employees. When confronted by the irate poet, an official was quoted in *The Independent* as saying, "People find poetry irrational and strange. They don't understand it. They're frightened by it."

The irony was that Swansea was to be a City of Literature in 1995. Jenkins had expressed disquiet about the concept long before the spat over the lapidary inscriptions. Unhappy at the exclusion of local writers, he had set up the Swansea Writers and Artists Group (SWAG) to remind the organisers of their existence. In the event, the year of literature proved little more than an exercise in civic philistinism and internecine strife among the literati. Jenkins also served as the first secretary of the Welsh Union of Writers, another campaigning group, but it had little clout with funding bodies.

He was a man of the Left, his political views finding expression in the ranks of Plaid Cymru, and he served on the editorial board of *Radical Wales*, though as a Welsh republican he sometimes groaned at the party's shortcomings. "It is difficult to write effective political poetry," he once told an interviewer, "in the same way that it must be difficult to write religious poetry, without banging the drum and thumping the tub. I have fallen into such error all too readily. On the other hand, there is scope for the political poem which may not have much of a shelf-life but which has a job to do, gets in there, blazes away and gets out again."

Nigel Jenkins was born in Gorseinon, Swansea, in 1949 and raised on his parents' farm in Gower. He worked for four years as a reporter in the English Midlands and then, after wandering in Europe and North Africa, and working as a circus-hand in America, studied comparative literature and film at Essex University. He returned to Wales in 1976, settling in Mumbles on Swansea Bay and earning a living as a freelance writer. With his rich voice, the blackest of beards and rugged good looks, he was a popular participant in readings and conferences. A kind, eirenic and selfless man, he was generous with others and especially so with younger writers, whom he encouraged and whose work he promoted.

He first came to prominence as one of three young poets named by the Welsh Arts Council in 1974. From the start his concern was with Wales and its place in the world. His poems are in turn local, cosmological, satirical, playful, bitter, comic, ribald, and dismissive. They are to be found for the most part in *Song and Dance* (1981), *Practical Dreams* (1983), *Acts of Union* (1990), *Ambush* (1998) and *Hotel Gwales* (2006). He also published two collections of haiku and senryu, namely *Blue* (2002) and *O for a Gun* (2007); the traditional Japanese forms lent themselves well to the concise wit and withering satire of which he was a master.

Two books of prose added to his reputation: *Gwalia in Khasia* (1995) is about Welsh missionaries in the Khasi hills of north-east India while *Footsore on the Frontier* (2001) brings together a selection of his miscellaneous essays. The first of these, selected as the Wales Book of the Year in 1996, was compared by competent critics to the work of such travel-writers as Jan Morris and Paul

Theroux. He also wrote a warmly appreciative monograph on John Tripp, a fellow-poet whose search for any sign of benevolent grace struck a chord with him.

Jenkins' theatre work included *Waldo's Witness* (Coracle, 1986), about the great pacifist poet Waldo Williams, and *Strike a Light!* (Made in Wales, 1989), about the Chartist and pioneer of cremation, Dr William Price. Two coffee-table books followed: *The Lie of the Land* (with photographer Jeremy Moore, 1996) and *Gower* (with David Pearl, 2009). He also edited the symposium *Thirteen Ways of Looking at Tony Conran* (1995), in homage to a poet he greatly admired, and served as one of the co-editors of *The Encyclopaedia of Wales* (2008). His two books on *Real Swansea* (2008, 2009) are a psychogeography of the "ugly, lovely" city which he knew in intimate detail.

THE INDEPENDENT 13 FEBRUARY 2014

Tribute to Nigel Jenkins 1949-2014

Plaid Cymru AM for South Wales West, Bethan Jenkins.

Nigel Jenkins , who died today at the age of 64, was one of Wales's most committed and also eclectic writers. He won many prizes, including Wales book of the year in 1996. He was a dedicated member of Plaid Cymru, and regularly emailed me with his thoughts and ideas about how Plaid Cymru could be active in helping to improve the area of South Wales West, as well as his views on the aspiration for a Republican Wales for the future.

He supported our local campaign in Swansea against the closure of the Dylan Thomas bookshop, and the campaign against any possible downgrading of the Dylan Thomas Centre in Swansea. He was a long-term activist in CND Cymru, and members of CND Cymru have contacted me to express their sadness at his death, in recognition of his activism.

He was an editor of the influential *Radical Wales* magazine, and very active in the Welsh Union of Writers. He learnt Welsh and was a great supporter of the Welsh language.

He will be sadly missed by all who care about literature and left-wing politics in Wales.

Plaid Cymru's Swansea West Assembly candidate Dr Dai Lloyd said:

"Nigel Jenkins was a poet whose work enlightened the life of the whole of Wales. He had the precious gift of helping us laugh at ourselves, in both our languages — but at the same time celebrating what our nation had to offer to the world.

"Like Dylan Thomas, whose centenary we mark this year, his poetry and scholarly prose publications placed Swansea, Gower and Wales on a world-wide stage.

"I was fortunate to have known him well — our children attended the same Welsh-medium schools and our paths often crossed, both politically and culturally.

"He will be sadly missed in the Swansea area in particular, but his unique voice lives on in his inspiring poetry."

PLAID CYMRU WEBSITE 28 JANUARY 2014

Tributes paid to 'major cultural and literary figure' Nigel Jenkins

Nigel Jenkins, associate professor of literature at Swansea University and award-winning poet, has died after a brief battle with cancer

Wales has lost a "major cultural and literary figure" following the death of multi-award winning Swansea poet, editor, journalist and broadcaster Nigel Jenkins, Dylan Thomas prize chairman Peter Stead said today.

Jenkins, 64, who lived in Mumbles, died early this morning after a brief battle against pancreatic cancer at Swansea's Ty Olwen hospice

He was brought up on a farm on the former Kilvrough estate in Gower and published several collections of poetry, including *Song and Dance* (1981), *Practical Dreams* (1983), *Acts of Union: Selected Poems* (1990), *Ambush* (1998) and *Hotel Gwales* (2006).

His collection of haiku and senryu, *Blue* (2002), was the first haiku collection ever to appear from a Welsh publisher, his second haiku collection, *O For a Gun*, was published in 2007.

He won the Arts Council of Wales 1996 Book of the Year prize with his travel book *Gwalia in Khasia* (1995) and published a selection of his essays and articles as *Footsore on the Frontier* (2001). He was co-editor of *The Welsh Academy Encyclopaedia of Wales*, published by the University of Wales Press in 2008. He was also the author of *Real Swansea*, (Seren Books, 2008) a personal account of the modern city, and *Gower*, (Gomer, 2009) and *Real Swansea 2* (Seren 2012).

An associate professor at Swansea University, he was the Co-Director of the university English department's creative writing programme.

The vice-chancellor Professor Richard Davies said: "Nigel's commanding presence was felt in the University far beyond his own department. For example, he wrote a graduation day celebration poem which has become an integral part of our graduation ceremonies. When he read the poem himself, it became a riveting drama."

The novelist Professor Stevie Davies, co-founder of the Swansea Creative Writing MA, described Nigel Jenkins as "an inspirational teacher, an outstanding writer and a true friend to authors, poets, dramatists and artists of all kinds throughout and beyond Wales.

"He was much loved by staff and students present and past, and we shall miss him greatly."

Broadcaster, historian and writer Peter Stead said after learning of his death today: "Wales and Swansea has lost a major cultural and literary figure in Nigel Jenkins.

"He was born on Gower and had deep roots in Swansea as evidenced in his lively Real Swansea books.

"I was on the panel when Nigel won Arts Council Book of the Year prize for his book about his travels in India... he was a wonderful writer and I thoroughly enjoyed his travel writing.

"It's terribly ironic that in DT100 when the world is celebrating the birth of a Swansea poet, right at the outset of the year we are having to come to terms with the loss of one of our best and most influential local writers.

"He was a great, inspirational figure for other writers, a real character and he will be hugely missed. It's a sad day for Swansea."

Former mayor of Swansea and councillor for Mawr in the Swansea Valley, Ioan Richard said: "I had known Nigel for about forty years following on from an evening of *Poems and Pints* at the Queens Hotel, Swansea, where he was then reading with Chris O'Neill.

"Discovering Nigel was like chancing upon a Curlew's secret nest, as his writing was like a fresh and rare egg shining its colours on a new Gower morning.

"He progressed to become a great master of the written craft and his loss is a great loss for Swansea and the wider literary world."

Robin Turner, WalesOnline, 28 January 2014

Tributes to Nigel Jenkins 1949-2014

Nigel Jenkins, who died on Tuesday 27th January 2014, aged 64, was one of the most influential literary figures that Wales has ever produced. Forever associated with the landscape of Swansea his reach went far beyond the Mumbles, and heartfelt tributes have been paid from India to Australia and, of course, all around Wales. Wales Arts Review *is deeply honoured to publish this collection of tributes to Nigel from his friends and admirers, of which he left an uncountable mass.*

Robin Ngangom

We, in the Khasi Hills, remember you with love and affection. Go in peace, Nigel Jenkins, to partake in the divine betel nut.

Fflur Dafydd

I knew Nigel from an early age, as he was a close friend of my mother's. Every now and then, he came to stay with us when they were discussing translations of her poetry, and the very first thing I remember about him is finding his voice incredible to listen to. Like music itself.

Many years later, he became my colleague at Swansea University, and we formed a friendship of our own. When he later became Director of Creative Writing, I couldn't have asked for a more understanding or supportive boss. (Not that Nigel would ever be comfortable with being considered as a 'boss'.) I can't think of a single event or launch where Nigel wasn't present — he would always be there, supporting people, supporting the arts, supporting creativity, and was adored by his students. Something interesting always happened in Nigel's class — there was hilarity, music, and near-nudity once! The rest of us could never compete. Every year, the students seemed to ask for more poetry, more Nigel. Right up until he became ill, he was inspiring people and introducing novice poets to new worlds, new ways of seeing things.

Nigel was a writer through and through. Even his emails were pure poetry, and very often, sharp satirical comedy. I can still remember the way he threw his head back to laugh when I told him I'd be requesting maternity leave again, a gesture which said — 'ah, that's a good way of getting more writing time!' (And he was right, of course.) I remember our countless conversations about his daughters and how proud he was of them: 'the best thing I've ever done with my life' — as he once told me.

It is impossible to stress just how much we'll all miss him at Swansea University. And yet, it will only be a fraction of the loss that will be felt by those closest to him, and also the loss that will be felt in years to come, by the whole of Wales. We have lost a great poet and writer but also a great personality. Luckily for us, words are able to preserve a personality, and within his poems we can still find that laugh, that warmth, that wit, that *Nigelness* — and it is a comfort to know that through reading him, we can still find him, and be close to him, time and time again.

John Davies

I first came to admire Nigel when I read the type-script of his *Gwalia in Khasia*. Who else, I wondered, can write such splendid prose? Here is his comment on flying above Bangladesh: 'Pincered between the lethal surges of the Bay of Bengal and the annual deluge of monsoon water, much of it draining off the Khasi Hills, these coastal Bangladeshis are seasoned precisians of life's murderous whimsicality.' And these were his feelings on meeting the couple who looked after the cemetery in which Thomas Jones (The Founding Father of Khasi Alphabets and Literature, as his gravestone describes him) is buried: 'All that separated these two survivors from the lethal poverty of Calcutta's homeless thousands was this ramshackle boneyard and a Welshman's grave.'

I was hugely proud that my commendation was printed on the cover of *Gwalia in Khasia*. I took the book with me when I visited Shillong. A waiter informed me that the book was being serialized in the local English-medium newspaper. I went to see the editor, who informed me that 'your archdruid is in town'. I visited the Polo Towers Hotel and had breakfast there with Dafydd Rowlands, T. James Jones and Tegwyn Jones. It was Nigel Jenkins, therefore, that led me to meet the head of Gorsedd y Beirdd not far from the borders of Tibet.

I was delighted to hear that Nigel, with Menna Baines, would be joining me as editors of *The Encyclopaedia of Wales*. (We were fortunate that Peredur Lynch also became part of the team.) Our task was to prepare two volumes each containing nearly a million words, work which took far longer than the two years originally allotted to it. During those years and during the additional ones, I am happy to confirm that, among all the editors, there was fruitful cooperation and friendship.

I was amazed at Nigel's capacity for hard work, and his skill in turning the turgid writings of some of our contributors into translucent sentences. Meeting him was always a delight; his superb deep voice created a wondrous sonority and his conversation was constantly amusing and imaginative. When working on the *Encyclopaedia*, we would send each other at least half a dozen e-mails a day, but I have hardly met him since the work's publication. Recently, I thought of going to Swansea to see him, but then came the dreadful news of his serious illness. To realize that I will never see him again is the cause of the deepest sadness.

Mike Parker

'So many in Welsh lit over yrs have cited Nigel Jenkins as someone who had inspired, helped, been kind to them. That, friends, is

222

success': the words from Kathryn Gray plopped into the muddy swirl of my Twitter timeline. I nodded in silent agreement, though the thought did flit across my mind that it seemed a faintly random sentiment for a wet, workaday Tuesday. The sucker punch truth that it was a 140-character obituary only dawned a few tweets later.

At 64, Nigel was too young to go. The fire still roared within; it burst out in his poetry, prose, politics, lecturing, psychogeography and music; it combusted all around him and brought light and merriment; it scorched even through the hallowed chambers of the *Encyclopaedia of Wales*, a project that ate seven years of his life as one of its editors, and which he wearily nicknamed 'Psycho'. His inability to stand the sickly cant of sanctioned public discourse brought both admiration and brickbats galore, none more piously hurled than when his bilious eulogy to 'Viscount No', George Thomas ('The Lord of Lickspit / The grovelsome brown-snout and smiley shyster') landed him on the front of *The Guardian* and booed on the letters page of the *Western Mail* for months on end. As ever, he was proved entirely right on that one.

The last time I saw Nigel was at a hugely convivial event in Aberystwyth rugby club to mark *Planet* magazine's fortieth birthday. There was music, poetry, prose and speeches from a glittering cast that included Ned Thomas, Jan Morris, John Barnie, Gai Toms, Jasmine Donahaye, Damian Walford Davies and Samantha Wynne-Rhydderch. As compere of the evening, I'd come up with the idea of ascribing a different planet to each performer, a conceit that became distinctly strained on occasion (Jan Morris, suffering an injured foot, hobbled up to the stage after my introduction, cast me with a baleful eye and murmured, 'Well, I certainly don't feel very Mercurial right now'). While some were highly tenuous fits, there was no question which planet to give to Nigel: Mars, the red planet, named after the Roman god of war, the near neighbour that's fascinated us for generations, famous for its eruptions, its volcanoes and its elliptical orbit. I cringe to recall this now, but my last words before bringing Nigel to the microphone were 'So, is there life on Mars? There certainly is!'

And now there isn't. The sky is a far darker place without him.

Ceri Wyn Jones

Many who pay tribute to Nigel Jenkins will be conscious of somehow doing justice to the man and his achievements, knowing it to be a gloriously impossible task. Many will also be at pains to deliver such tributes in terms as original and eloquent as those of the man they mourn, fully aware of the futility of such an undertaking. But all who do so will do so with tears in their eyes.

I first shared the stage with him at a poetry reading in Swansea in 1997 at an evening entitled 'Beirdd yn Dweud "Ie"/Poets Say "Yes"' in support of the campaign to establish a National Assembly in Wales. But it wasn't until I joined Gomer Press as an editor in 2002 that I really got to know him and came to appreciate how much more he was than the captivating verbal and vocal presence of the public performance.

Gomer will point to Nigel's great successes across a range of literary forms: the travel writing of *Gwalia in Khasia* (Wales Book of the Year 1995), the collections of essays like *Footsore on the Frontier* (2001), the poetry collections like *Hotel Gwales* (2006) and even the coffee-table collaborations like *Gower* (2009). But I will remember him too for his championing of new authors, along with his willingness to graft and campaign as part of a team, for example, as one of the three joint-editors of *Another Country: Haiku Poetry from Wales* (2011).

Yes, he was one of Gomer's greatest authors, but he was also one of Gomer's greatest friends.

Ifor Thomas

Profound shock to hear of the passing of Nigel Jenkins.

He was hugely helpful to me when first trying to make a place in the Welsh literary world, later I got to know him much better during my time in the Welsh Union of Writers where, as a founding member and chair, he was unerring in steering that ship through the choppy wash of conflicting egos. He imparted to the Union a gravitas it never deserved. He was generous to the less-well recognised writer, more likely to be encountered at a poetry reading given by an unknown as at some stellar event. And his readings, how extraordinary they were. The cowboy boots, jeans, sonorous voice — I never saw him deliver a dud.

Stevie Davies

Nigel was a great lover of sea-swimming, as I am. We used to haunt Rotherslade Beach, which he called the 'Plage Principale', and would compete annually to see how long we could keep swimming into October and November. Nigel would often talk of the sea and the sensation of boundlessness we experience there, the peaceful, cold 'oceanic feeling', at home in our little nook of the world.

I frequently noted our conversations in my diary — here is one excerpt, which led, through Nigel's memorable quotation, into a great landscape of meditation.

6 March 2012
Nigel & I talked about our wonder when we see the stars & sea 'in our moment' — boundless wonder at everything — an atom, a firmament — & he quoted from Pinter: 'Tender the dead' & sent me the quotation. Nigel has the most beautiful mind of anyone's I've ever known — he himself is a source of wonder to me — the firmament within. He helped expose the 3,000 year old Bronze Age causeway in the Bay — which used to be a fen. We spoke about our

moment within archaeological time.

This is the email Nigel sent later that day:

Here's the entire quotation, Stevie, from Pinter's play No Man's Land, *which Michael Gambon read at his memorial service:*

"I might even show you my photograph album. You might even see a face in it which might remind you of your own, of what you once were. You might see faces of others, in shadow, or cheeks of others, turning, or jaws, or backs of necks, or eyes, dark under hats, which might remind you of others, whom once you knew, whom you thought long dead, but from whom you will still receive a sidelong glance, if you can face the good ghost. Allow the love of the good ghost. They possess all that emotion ... trapped. Bow to it. It will assuredly never release them, but who knows ... what relief ... it may give them ... who knows how they may quicken ... in their chains, in their glass jars. You think it cruel ... to quicken them, when they are fixed, imprisoned? No ... no. Deeply, deeply, they wish to respond to your touch, to your look, and when you smile, their joy ... is unbounded. And so I say to you, tender the dead, as you would yourself be tendered, now, in what you would describe as your life."

Peter Finch

We were in a long room above a pub somewhere in Neath. Nigel was teaching a creative writing class and I was the guest. I was there to explain what sound poetry was. This was south Wales in the 1970s and there were edges out there to be pushed. Encouraged by Nigel I'd done a run of sonic recreations of Schwitters, Jandl and Cobbing and then finished with a blast of my own stuff. At the back someone evinced the opinion that this was all, actually, crap. A common perception. T.S. Eliot would be spinning in his grave if he knew. Dylan Thomas would be aghast. However, this didn't prevent one

226

of Nigel's more enlightened students from vocally disagreeing. It's not crap, it's good. No it isn't. Whap. There was a scuffle and then fists began to fly. God this poetry is exciting stuff, Nigel told me, as he leapt forward to separate the fighting pair.

And it was too. With Nigel there at the heart of it.

Throughout the rest of his long career Nigel kept himself there too. At the heart. Whatever else he became famous for — and there were a great many things — he still called himself a poet. First and foremost. For Nigel poetry was the same thing as blood.

Although never an avant gardist himself, not quite, he supported those who were. If there was an underdog out there, someone not getting the right treatment, someone neglected or grossly misunderstood then Nigel would be the man to champion their cause. He supported the work of extreme Welsh-Canadian concretist Childe Roland, for example, offering him readings, bringing him to Swansea, espousing his cause. He supported the successful bid to get that writer offered full membership of the Welsh Academy.

The mainstream was not where Nigel felt most at home and despite his not inconsiderable success out there at the top of the tree — the BBC, The Arts Council, the posher publishers of Wales — he never lost touch with the other way of carrying on.

In America they loved the sound of his voice. I was with him in upstate New York where he was fronting his poetry and music group Y Bechgyn Drwg. Dressed in Stetson, long black coat and cowboy boots he could have doubled for Johnny Cash. But it was the Richard Burton-like sonority of his voice that engaged his audience.

In the latter part of his life the haiku, that three line form, seemed to take the place of his longer verse work. He told me once, walking across Swansea Bay in early 2012, that he thought poetry had deserted him. I just haven't written much lately, he confessed. Does that mean you are no longer a poet, I asked? Certainly not, was the immediate reply.

We'd worked on psychogeography together. His *Real Swansea* was a great success. He'd followed it with *Real Swansea Two* and before he died had virtually completed *Real Gower*. We'd wandered Mumbles together doing research for my *Edging The Estuary*. Nigel was keen to show me the ancient roadways of Swansea, Celtic walkways that went out into the sea, wooden paths built millennia ago, unearthed by archaeologists and still magnificently there — except in the incoming tide we never found them. We turning in circles. Nothing. That non-finding, as Nigel later pointed out, was in itself a perfect psychogeographic act.

It'll be hard now not having Nigel out there on the other end of the phone and always ready to respond to emails. Like me he was a hater of Christmas and in the early days did almost everything he could to be in work away from it all while the festivities rumbled elsewhere. For many years we'd celebrate this fact by calling each other while the rest of the world was eating turkey. He'd known John Tripp well, had written the Writers of Wales volume about him. He was one of the few in Wales who'd followed the poetry wars of the 70s and was familiar with how verse was everywhere from Serbia to San Francisco. He also understood and valued the little magazine and the small press. He ran one himself, publishing unknowns and setting them against the prevailing mainstream tide. He knew who Wales's champions were, the real ones. He possessed one of those Hemingway devices, a built-in, shock-proof, shit detector. He knew who our chancers were. He tolerated them with ill-ease.

He valued our country and hated to see it maligned, mis-represented or misunderstood. He was patriot to the core.

Others better qualified than I can write about his place as a travel writer, peace protestor, editor, encyclopaedist, teacher, critic, essayist, prize-winner, associate professor, publisher, champion, linguist, administrator, walker, harmonica player, bon viveur, broadcaster and donkey-jacket wearer. The jacket, that one with the embroidered shoulders. He must have worn it for forty years.

Nigel, we'll miss you. We won't be able to replace you. You're an impossible act to follow.

Jon Gower

He taught me stuff, did Nigel.

He taught me, in one of his sharp and sassy triads, that the brewery horse at Welsh Brewers must have diabetes, judging from the piss they served. He taught me that it is possible to love a place so much that it becomes you. And he showed me, effortlessly and in so, well, gentlemanly a manner, how to live in a spirit of selflessness and complete generosity. That generosity was seemingly embodied in that voice of his. If a pint of Guinness ever had a voice then it would be Nigel's. Dark, velveteen, nourishing and deep. Resonant as ocean's undertow.

We all remember such a giving man. Goodwill, support for others, excellent karma, the deepest kind of wisdom and a ready wit flowed from him. He gave in person, over a pint of (proper) beer or a glass of his beloved Rioja, in e-mails that seemed as carefully worked as old-fashioned letters, via his Stakhanovite work on 'Cyclops', the *Encyclopaedia of Wales*, and through his books, which were always gifts, they truly were.

And in so many ways he taught me how to write. I once took an MA class for him and asked him what he normally taught. He explained, with a touch of diffidence, that he normally used his own *Gwalia in Khasia*, but stressed that I could use any book I liked. I remember how pleased he was when I said that I'd teach *Gwalia* too, and do so without notes as I knew it so well. I doubt if I was ever his peer, but this sort of peer-respect was the best way I could underline my regard for his impeccably researched book. The fact that I'm currently writing a book called *Gwalia Patagonia*, modelled on, and inspired by Nigel's Book-of-the-Year-winning account of the Welsh in the Khasi hills, serves only to underline his very real and abiding influence.

But let me be specific about those writing lessons. He taught me how to marshal material in the shape of lists, and his account of the business of naming names in India is a veritable master class. Read it and smile. He taught me how to hunt down the right word, too — the *ensorcelling* song of the curlew. He so often claimed the perfect, magical, soaring word. That's why, in my opinion, he was the guv'nor.

In a *Planet* review of Nigel's *Footsore on the Frontier* David Lloyd describes the essays therein as 'the product of a generous spirit and a probing intelligence; open to experience, drawn to detail, careful of abstraction or pretension, inventive in establishing subtle or surprising connections among disparate subjects. It's the product of a writer who wants his words to communicate.'

Yes, his words communicated but they also enraptured, enthralled and oft' times delighted the reader beyond measure. The books aren't just an expression of him, or a version of him, they are him: so, by reading them, with fresh delight, he will never really leave us.

Go well, teacher.

Benjamin Palmer

I knew Nigel Jenkins for little more than a year, but I'm certain that his positive impact on my life is going to last far longer than that. I joined Swansea University's Creative Writing MA as a relative newcomer to poetry, but Nigel's enthusiasm and encouragement rapidly transformed my initial curiosity into a true passion. During our tutorials he'd thrust piles of books into my hands, introducing me to a host of poets whose work soon informed my own. Among them was the Oklahoman, Louis Jenkins, who although they were not related, would affectionately refer to his Welsh poet-in-arms as

'Cousin Nigel'. Others included the Japanese haiku masters Matsuo Bashō and Kobayashi Issa, as well as many Welsh or Wales-based writers beloved of Nigel, like Tony Conran, Ken Jones and Christine Evans.

To the new arrival, poetry can sometimes feel more like a haunted mansion than a land of joyful discovery. With its convoluted and cobwebbed corridors, its ranks of hallowed personages scowling down from high walls, not to mention all those bizarrely-named creatures — dactyls, spondees and anapaests — going bump in the night, the study of poetry can give the novice more cause for fright than delight. But with Nigel, although learning the craft was demanding — as it should be — it was also a highly enjoyable process. Even the fiendish complications of Welsh strict metre, which Nigel jokingly nicknamed 'Welsh S&M', were more a challenge to be relished than a punishment. The fact that I still get such a kick out of attempting to write *cynghanedd* and *englynion* in English today — though nobody is forcing, or even asking me politely to do so — is testament to the lasting influence of Nigel's teaching.

On top of all this he was a lovely man: generous, down to earth, and gifted with a mischievous sense of humour. I consider myself hugely lucky to have known and learned from him. He will be deeply missed by all those whose lives he touched, including, I'm sure, many grateful Swansea University Creative Writing students past and present

David E. Oprava

When Nigel Jenkins passed on Tuesday morning I sent a message to Jon Gower that simply said, 'I feel it in the world and the weather.' The rain, squalls, wind, and general turbulence of the atmosphere that morning left most of Wales feeling as if we were under the ocean — below a gale, perhaps on a Gower beach, at the edge of the surf where the storm waves crash. All of us were trapped in this churning as bands washed across our small bricks and bones. I had to teach all day, just as Nigel had taught me for a number of years, and as the hours went by I felt a little ashamed that I was not completely there for my students. I was not there for the rest of the world either. I was somewhere out in the sea of thoughts who has riptides and currents of its own. Colours turned into feelings and sounds into memories as the day ebbed and flowed around its own particular *axis mundi* — that day's meaning, its soul. Hours later I came to the wine-laden conclusion that there was a palpable hole in this world and a glorious explosion into the next. I imagined all of his talent, grace, gentle kindness and ribald wit expanding beyond the speed of light, beyond the speed of life. And for the first time ever in my existence, I felt a little bit better about death. He now knows the answer to the question, 'why?' He is now infinite. Knowing this settled me in my cups, so close to sleep, and I did what Nigel had taught me. I wrote as clearly and simply as possible...

To Nigel
I'm jealous
of a sort
now you know
what comes beyond
each twist of your soul
is gifted there
and makes me

Menna Elfyn

Some will remember 2014 as the year we celebrated the birth of Dylan Thomas. But, for me the date will remind me that this was the year Nigel Jenkins died, a poet who did so much for Wales and for the literary world beyond its borders.

Poet, teacher, journalist, essayist, performer, campaigner, nationalist — his talents were many and inexhaustible. I first came to know him during the anti-apartheid period when the two of us would encourage our fellow poets in Wales to not allow the National Museum to use their work in an exhibition of photographs from South Africa. From that first meeting onwards we derived great pleasure from working together to further the cause of poetry. I translated his work into Welsh and he, in turn, translated my work into English.

He had the true instinct of a writer — a curiosity about the world — and a desire to change it for the better. In my opinion there isn't another poet of his generation who so completely managed to both crystallize and encompass his love of Wales in his work. His presence on stage was nothing short of mesmerising and I well remember a reading tour of America where people were forever comparing him with Dylan as that deep voice spoke of conviction and found the profound. One of the students who came to study at Trinity said he thought that one of the old Celtic gods must surely have returned to be embodied within him. He enchanted his students and I was fortunate enough to share the job of Director of Creative Writing with him for seven years. A golden age of joint understanding, with trips to Tŷ Newydd as the annual highlight. He was the driver, tutor and careful organiser.

The thing that made him such a rounded and complete person was the depth of his experience. I can still see the faces of students as he talked about his time with the circus, sleeping with a snake in his caravan. I'm not sure that the snake turned into snakes by the end of the session. He was a journalist in England before he returned to Wales, burning with desire to see a confident Wales, full of pride in itself. Apart from the volumes of poetry he published, winning the Book of the Year for *Gwalia in Khasia* in 1996 was an important boost for him. He was a humble man, one who didn't push himself centre stage and who was always supportive of others. That was shown, once again, when he was commissioned to create verses for the walls of a new building at Morriston Hospital. He shared the work with other poets. Once again we were in his shadow, the gentle giant of Gower.

It was a strange feeling to visit him at Tŷ Olwen Hospice on Monday afternoon, hours before his death. Even though one was aware that his earthly journey was about to end, it was difficult not to see him at the helm, leading others safely to their journey's end

Bryn Griffiths

There are so many memories of Nigel I now hold dear: sampling the many ales together in The Park and The Pilot, old pubs of distinction in Mumbles, where I might regale him with tall tales of seafaring — far out there, swinging south below Bora Bora, and maybe the Horn — while he would sit quietly with his wry smile and twinkle of eye. He always listened and encouraged. In the midst of a jest, he would gently remind me of the need to publish my own selected poems and add, 'And what about your memoir, Bryn?'

Then there were the nights when we dined, following a few ales, with our friend, Spencer, at Oystermouth's Indian restaurant, where we talked of Swansea and Gower, old and new; a subject always close to our hearts. Sometimes at Tŷ Llên with Margot we'd attend readings by poets known and unknown, some talented and some not, but many of whom had been helped and encouraged by Nigel. He did not seek the company of the famous.

There was once a day when the sun shone on Swansea, and at that time Nigel was researching his first *Real Swansea* volume. He'd asked me to contribute something about Swansea's East Side, and thus we set out that sunny morning, walking and conversing throughout the day, while making our way through the haunts and playgrounds of my childhood — Foxhole Road, St Thomas, the docklands, and across the now-buried slag heaps of White Rock copper works. The evening found us at a shiny new bar, in a glossy new building, adjacent to the old Prince of Wales Dock. The ale was fine, we agreed, but the architecture was crap.

It was a memorable day.

There was always a quiet grandeur about Nigel in the way he combined gravitas, kindness and wisdom within a strong frame, coupled with his abiding humour. He was of Arthurian stature in South-West Wales (although no admirer of any contemporary Camelot), and an intrinsic part of this Welsh community… now and for time to come.

I will miss him through all the days that remain to me.

WELSH ARTS REVIEW 30 JANUARY 2014

An open letter to
Pennard Community Council

IWA Director Lee Waters asks Pennard Community Council to treat the burial of poet Nigel Jenkins as an exceptional case

Open letter to Dr Margaret Waymark, Clerk to Pennard Community Council.

Dear Dr Waymark

Nigel Jenkins is to be buried on Monday. His last wish was to be laid to rest on the land in Pennard where he had once played as a child. As you know his family agreed to sell the land some time ago to benefit the whole community as a site for the Pennard Burial Ground. It seems a cruel irony that this act may well see him denied his final wish.

As one of Wales' pre-eminent modern poets and cultural figures, Nigel's association with the Gower was not a superficial, or a passing one. He we wrote widely about the rich history and heritage of the area, and lived, until his untimely death last week, just a few miles away.

Despite a huge number of emails to the community council to ask you to reconsider your refusal to allow Nigel to be buried in Pennard, you have issued a defiant statement restating your position that:

"there is a policy in place which was set out in order to ensure that Pennard Burial Ground remains open and available to residents for as long as possible. The policy, on this basis, was set many years ago that only those resident within the ward be eligible. The Council has a duty to treat every case impartially and to see that everybody is equal in death. There have been many exceptions sought and declined over the years and these families would unfortunately have been just as disappointed. We would also like to point out that, in addition to the standard response, every democratic avenue to make an exception was explored. Unfortunately, in this instance, it was the settled will of the majority of councillors that no exemptions be made to policy on the grounds of consistency."

In response the National Poet of Wales, Gillian Clarke has written asking you to reconsider to allow a shocked and grieving family to fulfil Nigel's wish to be buried on his childhood land. In answer to your statement she wrote:

"Rules? There must be rules, but there must always be exceptions to rules in a civilised society. This permission, if granted, would not become a precedent, as there is no other Pennard poet needing burial on his ancestral land. The writers of Wales are gathering in their grief, and it is their collective request that this rule be set aside.

"Please listen. Poets, and poetry lovers, will respect Pennard, will visit, will remember and will pause to spend a quiet moment of grief and gratitude to a place that can only increase its reputation for being civilised if you change your minds."

Indeed, both the local AM, Edwina Hart, and the local MP, Martin Caton, have joined forces to ask you to show some compassion in applying your own rules in this case. In a letter to you they wrote: "Nigel Jenkins was a cultural and literary figure in Wales and beyond; his work has been translated into French, German, Hungarian, Dutch and Russian. Or to put it another way: Mae hen wlad fy nhadau yn annwyl i mi, Gwlad beirdd a chantorion enwogion o fri…(Land of my Fathers, So dear to me, A land of poets and minstrels, famed people)…

It would be a great shame if the words of our national anthem do not hold true for the late Nigel Jenkins in the land of his fathers."

It strikes me that you may not have fully understood the depth of feeling that your decision would awaken. Far from being an act of weakness to respond to such feeling, I believe it would be seen as a mark of compassion and respect. It would not set a precedent for other cases as the circumstances are so unique.

Nigel is due to be buried within the churchyard at St. Mary's Pennard on Monday. The former Archbishop of Canterbury, Rowan Williams, is among many who are praying for a last minute change of heart to allow Nigel Jenkins to rest where he once played without care.

Regards

Lee Waters

Nigel Jenkins was buried on 10th February 2014, at St. Mary's Pennard

THE WELSH AGENDA 6 FEBRUARY 2014

Farewell to poet who held close his vision for Wales

John Osmond reports from Pennard where Nigel Jenkins was laid to rest on Monday.

Nigel Jenkins, much loved bard of Gower and Wales, choreographed his own funeral as performance art. Held on Monday at St Mary's Church in Pennard in the Gower, just yards from the family farm where he was brought up and rode horses as a boy, he planned the event down to the last detail.

For the hundreds who attended, most of them in the nearby Community Hall where sound of the ceremony was relayed, the proceedings were as much if not more an artistic spectacle than a religious occasion.

It began with the wicker coffin being carried on six shoulders from the hearse into the thirteenth century church to the mournful sound of Peter Stacey's Breton pipes. But as we entered the church the clouds parted and the sun shone.

Inside it was as though we were transported into an eighteenth century revival, the place crammed and even the gallery above full beyond the tolerance level that modern-day health and safety rules allow. We sang Joseph Parry's *Myfanwy* and, to Andy Jones' guitar accompaniment, Idris Davies' *Bells of Rhymney*. There were poems and readings. The eulogy was delivered by cousin Noel Witts who 64 years ago, when he was 11-years old, became Nigel's 'Uncle'.

One of the readings, was a recording of Nigel's own unforgettable baritone voice in a rendering of some of his best lines 'Where poems come from' (you can hear them on Youtube). Wynn Thomas, a friend and colleague at Swansea University, read another of his poems, 'Is that where they make clouds, Dad?' —

It is beautiful, the filth gusting
From a stack at Baglan, turned by the late sun
To a wing of silver
Rising against
The blackly green, languorous hills;
Beyond the great dapplers bundling east,
An unearthly simplicity of open sky;
Here at our feet the tide bangs in,
Loud lengths of it slapping
The concrete steps.
There could be rain. There will be night.

Finally, to the strains of a Bach partita, played on unaccompanied violin by Ivor McGregor, the coffin was lifted once more and carried outside. At the graveside, after the coffin was slid into the ground, glasses were passed round to the family and champagne poured. "What champagne do you want, Dad?" Nigel was asked. "The best," he replied.

Nigel, of course, meant most to the very many people across Wales and beyond who knew and, invariably, were influenced by him. He had an acute sense of our lives being lived through what his great friend Osi Rhys Osmond, a painter poet, has described as our "brief eternities". In a tribute on the WalesArtsReview website, novelist Stevie Davies, who along with another friend, poet Menna Elfyn, also read at the funeral, quoted from a diary entry she made:

6 March 2012
Nigel & I talked about our wonder when we see the stars & sea 'in our moment' — boundless wonder at everything — an atom, a firmament — & he quoted from Pinter: 'Tender the dead' & sent me the quotation. Nigel has the most beautiful mind of anyone's I've ever known — he himself is a source of wonder to me — the

firmament within. He helped expose the 3,000 year old Bronze Age causeway in the Bay — which used to be a fen. We spoke about our moment within archaeological time.

Nigel will live on in such memories and, of course, through his poetry and other writings. It is entirely fitting that he now lies close to the graves of two other poets he much admired, Vernon Watkins and Harri Webb. Despite its Community Council, Pennard is blessed indeed.

But what ultimately was important about Nigel, and why so many people were touched by his life and early death was that, at a critical time, in the mid-1970s, he chose Wales. And in making that choice, he came to learn that choosing Wales also means making Wales. And that he proceeded to do, in his inimitable, painstaking, and grafting way over decades.

He was intensely local, as his two books about 'Real Swansea' demonstrate, and as his posthumous volume on 'Real Gower' will reiterate. But he also held close, but shared with gusto, a vision of Wales as a whole. That's why we remember him.

THE WELSH AGENDA 12 FEBRUARY 2014